DEDICATION

This book is dedicated first to Sgt. Steve Clement, Lt. Roy Richardson, Sgt. John Gutekunst, Specialist Peter Nolan, Specialist Wayne Smith, Specialist Steve Golsh, Specialist Louis Barbaria, and PFC. Gary Manchester, as well as many more brothers-at-arms that served and were killed in the Vietnam War.

Secondly, this dedication goes to my wife Jackie, my best friend, who has put up with me for 43 years and thirdly to our sons, Dan & Mike and their families who have enriched our lives and brought us much joy.

A RELUCTANT WARRIOR'S
Vietnam Combat Memories

Printed in the United States of America
Triune Group, Inc. – Publishing Division
Library of Congress Number Pending

Copyright © September 30, 2014
By Richard L. McBain
All Rights Reserved

ISBN-13: 978-1502586018
ISBN-10: 1502586010

ABOUT THE AUTHOR

Richard L. McBain, 65, was drafted into the Army in early 1969 while attending college. After his combat infantry training, he was assigned to the 101st Airborne Division in Vietnam, and served with Alpha Company, $2/502^{nd}$ Infantry in Northern I Corps. He was awarded two Bronze Stars, one with V Device, as well as the Purple Heart, Air Medal, Army Commendation Medal, VNS, VNC, NDS and Good Conduct medals, with a Presidential Unit Citation, and his most prized award, the Combat Infantryman's Badge. He has been a business executive for over 30 years, a husband to Jackie for 42 years, father to Dan and Mike, and grand-father to Nathan, Cade, Mattie, and Carter. He is the author of seven other published books.

TABLE OF CONTENTS

Dedication	1
About The Author	3
Table of Contents	4
Prologue	6
Chapter One – Deadly Toss of a Coin	9
Chapter Two – Oh No!	14
Chapter Three – Arriving in the Nam	30
Chapter Four – Christmas Operations	41
Chapter Five – Combined Operation with ARVN'S	60
Chapter Six – Stand-down?	69
Chapter Seven – Kit Carson Scout – Ton Lon Diep	87
Chapter Eight – 2nd Five O 'Deuce – Strike Force	98
Chapter Nine – Incoming	107
Chapter Ten – Drugs in Vietnam	118
Chapter Eleven – Operations for a Body Count	124
Chapter Twelve – Friendly Fire	136

Chapter Thirteen – Eagle Beach	149
Chapter Fourteen – Combat Assault	161
Chapter Fifteen – Battle for Hill 882	178
Chapter Sixteen – A Break from the Fight - R&R	193
Chapter Seventeen – Huge Mistake - Almost	200
Chapter Eighteen – Replacements	208
Chapter Nineteen – Combat Squad Leader	213
Chapter Twenty – Battalion Radio Operator	233
Chapter Twenty-One – A Huge Surprise	244
Chapter Twenty-Two – Home from Viet Nam	257
Chapter Twenty-Three - Brothers in Battle	270
Other Brothers in our Unit	285
Epilogue	303
Vietnam War Glossary	304
Some Vietnam Statistics	307
Acknowledgements	312

PROLOGUE
by Dick McBain

The Sixties and early Seventies were indeed quite unlike anything that had been seen before. Teenagers and young adults were rebelling by the tens of thousands in cities and Universities across America. Manners and parental respect were being replaced by selfishness and the drive to feel good, including the proliferation of drug use. Music was written to reflect the signs of the times and against a very unpopular war. Demonstrations were being held in the streets by thousands, and whole campuses and their Administration Buildings were being taken over by students in protest for the Vietnam War. What was most amazing was that for the first time the war and all of the demonstrations could be seen on the evening news and in real time.

The rebellion brought about the Hippie Movement which was supposedly established for love and freedom. Boys and men with long hair clashed with the construction industry work force who thought it disgraceful for men to look like women. "Normal" families had their dysfunctions made public, and middle-America seemed to be on the brink of collapse.

I was the middle sibling of five with a brothers and sister on either side of my age. I was brought up in Catholic, middle-class neighborhoods in the suburbs of Cleveland, Ohio, by a doting mother and a father, who had returned four years prior` to my birth from WWII in Europe. My Dad went in on Omaha Beach on D-day and was a surgical assistant during the war.

The value system I learned from my parents and my Catholic school upbringing would follow me up and through the war. I learned to love and serve God, be a man of my word, and exhibit integrity where ever I went. I was a died-in the-wool patriot and believe to this day in God, Honor, and Country. My value system was instrumental in understanding that there are things more important in life than personal aspirations and desires.

One of those things was the call to serve during the Vietnam War. I did not believe that the Vietnam War was good or necessary, but I did believe that if your country calls you have a duty to something that ranks higher than personal opinions or fears. I had prayed with the rest of my family for my older brother John who served in the Army in Vietnam a couple of years before I was called. Like most families, especially those with members in the war, I watched the news regularly for information on the war's progress, and to make sure my brother's unit was ok.

When I returned from the jungles, I joined in the family communication with our Congressman asking him to redirect my younger brother Bob to another duty station. Bob had entered Basic Training while I was in Vietnam, and everyone felt that two out of three brothers was enough for this fight, not to mention my Dad's time in WWII. The Congressman agreed with us and managed to get Bob a duty station in a mobile medical unit in Germany, they called a MUST Unit. We were all very pleased and although Bob was more than prepared to go to Vietnam, we felt that two was enough.

The horrors of war are not something most people will be able to understand unless they have been there. I, like so many thousands and thousands were abruptly taken from a peaceful civilian life and within a few months of training found ourselves in big firefights with an enemy trying to kill us. We continued to see buddies shot or blown apart, that ten minutes earlier were describing what their home was like and expecting a return to it.

In the book I describe a battle for a hill that my platoon of 45 men began, and after two weeks of fighting only three were left available for duty. Most of the men were wounded and several killed, which required a new start with fresh replacements from the United States.

The stamina of men and women in war zones is more than any of them think they have. The freedom and life we have in America is the main reason so many of us have this dedication to duty and responsibility to do our part when needed. The United States is indeed the envy of the world, even though many may not admit it, but we Americans need to be careful not to take all of the blessings we have for granted, as we can easily see so much of the world is in dire need.

In conclusion, I want to state how proud I am to have served my country in a very difficult time, but lament my brothers and sisters at arms that paid a dear price, both with their lives or wounds that may never heal. God Bless America!

CHAPTER ONE

DEADLY TOSS OF A COIN

"Nine ball in the corner pocket", said Steve Clement, as we were finishing up a game of pool. Our company had been brought in to Camp Eagle for a two-day stand-down, and Steve and I went to a hooch in the rear of our company area to play some pool. One of the few amenities for the limited number of times we would find ourselves in the rear area was the pool table and the enlisted men's club, so called.

Sgt. Newton "Steve" Clement was Dick's best friend and suffered a terrible and unnecessary death in an ammo dump explosion due to some "Cherry" playing around.

Steve Clements was a tall, 21 year old buddy of mine, who happened to be the first guy I met when I reported to my platoon earlier in the year. He had just been married before coming over to Vietnam, and had a baby on the way. Steve was a mild mannered man who was folksy and very easy to like. He would do anything for you, and never expected anything in return. He was a guy I just liked to be around, and we made as much fun as we could in a lousy situation.

Steve and I had a thing going that whenever one or the other would make hot chocolate or coffee in the boonies, the other would come around with our noses in the air saying, "What are we having that smells so good?"

Sergeant Manning came into the hooch and said, "OK guys, get your gear together, we're making a CA (combat assault by helicopter) to this side of the A Shau Valley". "Oh common Top, we just got in yesterday", I said in an irritated voice. "Yeah, what happened to our two day's", Steve chimed in. "Stop you're belly aching", Top said, "and get your stuff together. I don't make the orders, I just see you do them. Now get going; you move out in one hour". Top Manning walked out of the hooch leaving Steve and I ranting about being screwed again by the "Green Machine". "Man, what is the deal anyway, are we ever going to get a real rest without it being interrupted?" I asked.

It had become just common place that our very infrequent two-day stand-down's were always interrupted either early, meaning we were sent out on another mission before they ended, or with training exercises that the Army would use to keep us out of mischief.

"You want to get the ammo or C-rations", Steve asked. "Makes no difference to me", I said with a shrug of my shoulders. "Let's flip for it", Steve replied. "OK, but I'll call it", I said. Steve pulled out a quarter and flipped it in the air. "Heads", I called out as the coin dropped to the table. Heads it was! "I guess I'll get the C-rations and ruck sacks", I said, simply because they were all located in the company area. That meant Steve had to go farther to an ammo dump to pick up the ammo and claymore mines. "Guess I'll get the ammo then", he said smiling knowing he had no other choice. "See ya in a few", Steve said walking out of the door. I never realized those would be the last words I ever heard from my friend.

I went out to the supply area to get the C-rations and our gear together, and began to pack our rucksacks with this wonderful canned crap they called food. Top had given us very little details about where we were going or what we would be doing, so I wasn't sure if there was anything else we were going to need for the mission. After loading the C-rations and filling a few canteens, I closed up the rucksacks waiting for Steve to get back so we could finish.

All of a sudden a tremendous explosion shattered the air. "KA-BOOM".... followed by hundreds of explosions and bullets going off and...."fffffffsshhhhhhhh", rockets shooting off. Grenades, rockets, and every other kind of ordinance began falling all over the company area and us. "What in the world" I began to say when the most terrible thought came to my mind. "The ammo dump...the ammo dump's exploding...Steve's up there...Steve's up there", I was yelling at the top of my lungs. Explosions were raining down all around us, and we were trying to find cover, running in this direction and that, in total confusion.

Doc Shenk, our platoon medic was a friend who had grown particularly close to Steve and me. As I was yelling about Steve, Doc was already on his way up the hill to the ammo dump while it was exploding. He and many of our medics continually put themselves in harm's way running to wounded men under fire, and braving explosions to get to them.

He found Steve, who had been blown to the side of the hill, bleeding and in horrible shape. Doc drug Steve down the hill away from the main explosions, and began to work on him. Doc found himself that day, like many of us had in other situations, numb as he worked feverously trying to stop the bleeding and save his close friend.

Doc Bill Shenk, a dear friend and one of the bravest men I knew, continually running out under fire to get to his wounded brothers. A real Medic!

The carnage lasted a good twenty minutes until there was just an occasional explosion. There was still unexploded ordinance all around the area, and we had to be very careful where we were walking. The engineers were walking around with certain safety gear picking up the unexploded ordinance and stowing it in safety containers. I thought that what they were doing was something that I would not do, but then again, someone had to get it done.

We were later in a group around the orderly room trying to get information about Steve before we left, but there was nothing anyone could tell us. We did know from Doc

Shenk that it did not look good for him, and that he was in a very bad way.

The mission departure time was delayed a few more hours, and we were restricted to our company area so we would not be wounded by the explosives lying all around us. We heard that Steve was in a comma, and severely burned all over his body. Days later we were told that he never regained consciousness.

Steve Clement died two days after the explosion from his wounds. I was shaken quite a bit, not only because I lost a dear friend, but also because I realized that a toss of a coin decided which of us would be killed that day. I had been in the jungle now for seven months, and my experiences left me wondering if I would make it out alive, especially with what had just happened to Steve.

I sat down leaning up against my rucksack waiting for our orders to move out, and thought back to what started all of this for me.

CHAPTER TWO

OH NO!

It was March of 1969 and I opened the letter from the draft board and read the all too familiar start of an induction notice. "Greeting! You are hereby notified of your induction to military service..." I was still not too worried because of what the doctors had told me a few months before about my brain injury.

Back in December I was home from college and was down at a beer bar at the University of Dayton. Many of my friends were coming in that day from their colleges for the holidays, and this was one of our favorite meeting places. My younger brother Bob came down after work at about 11:00 p.m., and was jumped by a local gang outside of the bar known as the Brown Street Gang.

A couple of guys came running up to me in the bar yelling the Brown Street Gang has got your brother outside. Without another word I headed for the door and felt pretty wasted from all of the beer I had been drinking. I ran out side with a sizeable group of friends and other spectators following to see what was going on. There was a sheet of ice on the parking lot which made the going even worse. They had a small circle around him and their leader was inside the circle fighting my brother Bob.

I busted through the circle and ran up hitting their leader hard and knocking him down. Instead of fighting the man I hit, I turned to my brother to see if he was Ok. The guy got up and nailed me from behind and I felt my feet go out from under me as I slipped on the ice and fell. The gang surrounded me and began kicking me, and evidently one of them landed a solid kick to the temple area of my head, and I was out.

My friends and brother saw what happened and heard the crack of my skull, so they all jumped in and fought the gang off. They put me in a car and I lay in my brothers' lap going through periods of not seeming to breathe, to vomiting all over the place. I spent the days leading up to Christmas in and out of a coma, and my hospital room became a meeting and party place for many of my friends, who would sneak up the back stairs in the hospital. I came out of it a couple of days before the holiday.

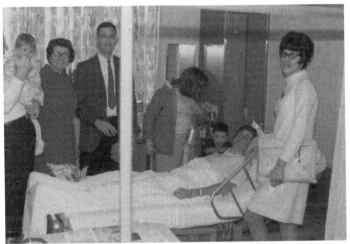

Dad holding Shelly, Mom, Mike, Ginny, Tommy, Me & Gail when I came out of a coma on Christmas Day from my head being kicked in a week prior

I had some brain damage and my family doctor told me I would not be able to be drafted as a result. When I received my draft notice, I waltzed down to my family doctors office for a meeting, and to get a letter to send to the draft board. "I can't write the letter to keep you out Dick", he told me very nonchalantly. "What do you mean, Doc", I said angrily, "You told me I had brain damage and that it would keep me out of the military", I protested. "Dick, you've healed miraculously, and we can't keep you out now", he explained. "Dr. Kelso, I still have no sense of smell or taste...what do you mean healed", I fought back. "Those senses aren't enough to keep you out...we thought you were going to have many more problems and you don't", he responded. After a volley of barbs back and forth, I steamed out of his office, never to see him again professionally.

I was to leave for the military on March 19, 1969, but wanted to finish the quarter at Sinclair College first. During the Vietnam War they had a two-year enlistment, and all enlistments gave you up to one hundred and twenty days to delay your start time. I went down and enlisted for two years so I could get the delay time to finish the quarter. Shortly after enlisting, I quit going to school because I was upset about going into the military, and convinced myself that I should have all the fun that I could before going.

June 19, 1969, I rode the bus from downtown Dayton to Cincinnati to the induction center. I went through my final testing, and physical. It was one of the loneliest day's I remember in my life, but was broken up when my brother-in-law, Mike McDonough, showed up to take me to lunch. He'll probably never know how that helped me get through the rest of that day's depression.

When I went into the doctor who made the final physical decision, he asked me if I had anything to report. "Not really", I replied, "Except I had a brain injury last December, and have no sense of taste or smell". "No sense of taste or smell", he asked incredulously, "that's brain damage", he said. I thought "Duh" but trying to be forthright I said, "My doctor said it was not enough to keep me out of the military"! He stared at me in silence for about thirty or forty seconds, then grabbed a red stamper and said, "Well, if you want to go into the military that badly...", and stamped my papers accepted. I tried to protest quickly seeing his uncertainty, "Wait...", "Next", he shouted as I was shown the way out by a Sergeant at the door.

After all of the physicals were accomplished, we were led into a flag draped room to be sworn-in. Now I was still reeling from the debacle with the doctor realizing if I had played my words differently, I may have easily been disqualified. I realized the moment had passed never to return, so I raised my right hand and swore my allegiance and commitment to a country I very much believed in, realizing it would take me to a war I very much did not believe in.

The emotions were quite mixed. I was proud to become a soldier and have the chance to serve my country as my father had done in WWII, and my older brother John in Vietnam a year or so earlier, but I did not want to die for such a foolish war. Anyway, the die had been cast, and for better or for worse I was now in the Army.

We were then bussed to Cincinnati Airport, where I was about to take my first commercial flight. I was seated next to a guy named Montessi, from Cincinnati, and he was like me...feeling the blues...going into the Army...and taking his first flight. We started talking about how the plane took off, and other things we knew nothing about. We then discussed music that we both loved. We found a common favorite song in our talk, "One" by the Three Dog Night. Every time Montessi and I would run into each other in basic training, whoever saw the other first would sing out, "One is the loneliest number that you'll ever do", which was the first line of the song.

We landed in Philadelphia, and boarded the buses that would take us to Fort Dix, New Jersey for basic training. We arrived at Ft. Dix about 9:45 pm or so, and our first orders came. "Fall out and line up beside the bus" a Sergeant yelled. It was dark outside and they picked a few of us to be Road Guards. As such, I had to put on a florescent vest, was given a flashlight, and every time we neared a road intersection, the road guards would run ahead of the company and take up position in the intersection holding back any traffic until all were through.

They were taking us to a mess hall to be fed, as we hadn't had anything but a snack on the plane since lunch. After a quick meal we were marched to an old WWII two story barracks, where we took a bunk and slept till morning. Since we had arrived so late, they let us sleep until 6:30 am, oh sorry, I meant 0630 hours. After breakfast we were marched to the barber shop for our haircuts. Now I had always like to joke around in my life, so I looked at the barber as I sat in his chair and said, "Just a little off the top and leave the sideburns". Unfortunately he was not amused, and simply stated, "Ok wise guy!" I knew I was in for it then. He scalped me, and not easily, it actually hurt. One of the guys had a huge Afro, which was like a ball of hair about a foot and a half out from his head. When they were finished with him he looked like an entirely different man and we all laughed in good heartedness about the drastic change.

We then were marched over to a warehouse where we lined up and were issued a duffel bag where we stuffed our uniforms and field gear they were giving us. We spent the next day or so stowing our civilian clothes, labeling everything and anything issued to us, and learning to spit shine our boots. During this time we were shouted at a few times, but I thought things weren't nearly as bad as I had expected. Then came the day!

We were told to fall out with everything we had, lined up in ranks which they had already shown us how to do, and marched over the where we were going to begin our real training. As we approached this large parking lot, there were about six or seven Drill Sergeant's standing in line about six feet apart. They had their Smokey the Bear hats tilted down over their eyes, and their uniforms were starched and pressed to the tee. Once they accepted the transfer of us from the Replacement Station guys, our world changed immediately.

"Ok you maggots, get your asses over here in this area and fall in", was yelled by the Field First Drill Sergeant. He voice shook the air and we were all falling all over ourselves to get across the curb and into the field area, while continuous yelling at the top of their lungs was coming from the other Drill Sergeants. "Move, move, move, move, what the hell is wrong with you morons, get going, get going, move, move, move", they were all shouting at the same time, while grabbing guys and shoving them in this direction and that, and it was very nerve racking as I'm sure it was meant to be.

Once we were in an acceptable formation, the Field First Sergeant, a black man who was a little older than the other Drill Sergeants, and seemed much more refined, spoke to us in a very calm voice.

"Ok dear hearts", he said using a term he would use throughout our training, "we are going to pick up all of our stuff and move out, and I mean fast up the stairs to your assigned rooms where you will drop your gear on your bunks and get your asses back down here in two minutes. Do you understand me?" he asked. "Yes Drill Sergeant" we yelled back loudly, having already been taught in the replacement center how to respond to a Drill Sergeant. "I can't hear you", was his response. "Yes Drill Sergeant", we yelled back again as loud as we could.

"Ok, move out", he commanded. "Move, move, move you maggots, you low life's, get moving, faster , faster, faster", came the loud yelling from the other Drill Sergeants as they ran alongside of us, pushing and shoving. God help us if we dropped an item or two as several did, which brought a couple of Drill Sergeants on either side of them where they pushed the trainee back and forth while they were trying to pick up their stuff during continuous yelling. I saw some of the guy's breakdown and cry during these moments which happened all throughout training, which was another mistake as there was no mercy for criers; just more harassment.

Basic training was a real black period in my life! I was miserable, lonely, demoralized, and tired most of those eight weeks. Ft. Dix, New Jersey, which was referred to as the "Country Club" as far as training sites go. The barracks were relatively new, but the breaking down of the civilian attitudes by the Drill Sergeants was very hard on me, albeit necessary as I realized later.

My friends were all out of college for the summer, and had planned to visit me after attending some concert in New York. They never showed up as the concert they attended was Woodstock, and they never imagined it would go on for three days. I was very disappointed when they didn't show up, but hey, you're in the Army now.

Dick at basic training. His brother John, recently home from Vietnam and still in the Army took the first shot with the peace sign, and Dick's basic training Army picture, while he was wearing fatigue pants that can't be seen

The fourth week while training on the rifle range with M-14's, one of my "roommates" named Dennis was in the foxhole next to me. Denny looked just exactly like Alfred E. Newman, the drawn character on the cover of Mad Magazine; I mean just like him. He was a funny guy who was always cracking jokes and telling stories about the Cadillac he was going to get so he would be able to "Drive in style".

Now Dennis could get rattled with the Drill Sergeants yelling, and they weren't supposed to be allowed to yell while on the range for just such reasons. Dennis was in the foxhole next to me and was having some trouble firing. His Drill Sergeant came running at him yelling, "You moron, what the hell is a matter with you", were his rants but he was not able to finish. Denny pointed that loaded M-14 at the Sergeant and said, "You got two seconds to run like hell before I blow your head off". The Drill Sergeant simply turned and ran like hell.

That night, I was awakened by noises outside, and looked out of my second story window in the barracks to see what was going on. Three Drill Sergeants were hovering over Denny on the black top, kicking him and yelling orders to low crawl across the parking lot. When I woke up the next morning, Dennis was gone. He went AWOL in the night and we never heard from him again.

My Drill Sergeant was named Manning from Georgia. He had returned from combat in Vietnam with the First Air Cavalry Division and was a tough guy, as were all of the Drill Sergeants. After the fourth week of training, we were at the rifle range completing our firing training, and during the test the Drill Sergeants had bet money on whose platoon would have the most "Expert" shooters, which was the highest shooting award in the Army. It tuned out that two platoons were tied for first place, and as I finished being the last shooter, Sergeant Manning came running to me. "McBain, what did you fire", he yelled at me. "Expert Sergeant!" I replied, as he ran up and picked me up in a hug off the ground dancing around, while the other Drill Sergeants gave me the evil eye.

After the fourth week of training, we were given our first weekend pass. A roommate of mine, Bill Messerschmitt, was picked up by his parents and asked me to come along. They lived on a farm in "Amish" Pennsylvania, and had some huge Clydesdale horses they raised. The farm was way out in the country, and so nicely quiet after such a nerve racking four weeks of training.

Bill and I did some bailing of hay in one of their fields, which was something I had done back home in Ohio as a seasonal job for our school bus driver who had a farm.

Dick and Bill Messerschmitt on Bill's family farm in Pennsylvania Dutch country. They raised Clydesdale Horses, and their neighbors who were Amish would drive their buggies up and down the road with the clip-clop of their horse hooves

Bailing hay was always good exercise and being in a farm field around horses brought back memories of home.

The fifth week of training I noticed a difference in the way the Drill Sergeants acted toward us. They continued their yelling and demanding a very loud, "Yes Drill Sergeant", in any response we gave them, but they had been able by that time to get to know us, and it seemed a little toned down from the first four weeks.

We received one other pass, and a few of us took a bus to Asbury Park, New Jersey, filled the tub with beer and ice, and had a great weekend. Gary Manchester and Eddie McLaughlin were both from Maine, as were a third of our basic training company. We enjoyed hanging around the beach and the amusement park there, and talking about our civilian life. Gary had been in college I think like myself, while Eddie was twenty-seven and a school teacher. Twenty-seven was the highest age they could draft you at the time, and he and a number of our guys were teachers from Maine that felt they really got a raw deal. Most of them were married and some with kids, which made it even more difficult for them.

Graduation from Basic Training was a day I enjoyed. It was a beautiful mid-August day, and the Army Band was playing while we all marched in dress uniforms before the base officers and family and friends in the bleachers, who were able to make it.

We received our orders and a large number of our company was going to clerk school, including Eddie McLaughlin and the other teachers from Maine. I was ordered to report to infantry training immediately, and left the next day along with Gary Manchester and a few other friends from "Basic". Bill Messerschmitt received orders for the Army Band, which was wonderful as he was an accomplished musician.

I arrived at Fort Lewis near Seattle in Washington State for infantry training. Joe Mazza, a guy from New Jersey which he would joke and call "New Guernsey", and I met there, and became friends. We would pal around on the base on weekends if we could get off duty, and just hang out. Sometimes I would go to the Enlisted Man's Club, where I would play drums with a couple of guitar players, and even put on a show one weekend.

Now in Basic we had fired the M-14, but here we would use the M-16, with which I also tested as expert. We were also trained with many weapons and things like trip flares, claymore mines, M-60 machine guns, M-79 grenade launchers and LAW's (light antitank weapons) rocket launchers.

I had caught a cold or sinus infection and went on sick call the day the company went to the range to fire the LAW. After being examined and getting a prescription, I was driven out to the range where everyone was finishing up. As we were assembled, an officer asked if anyone had not fired the LAW. I raised my hand and he instructed some Sergeant to take me out on the range and fire it. "Sir, I haven't had the training because I was"; he cut me off. Get out there and fire that thing. I told the Sergeant as we walked up to the firing line that I had been on sick call that morning, and didn't know anything about the LAW. "I'll show you", he said, "don't worry".

I was handed a LAW, and he said, "Ok, open it up"! "I don't know how Sergeant", I replied. The officer in the tower yelled through the speaker system "Hurry up and get him done". With that, the Sergeant grabbed the LAW, pulled the pins to remove the caps, extended the tube and handed it to me. "Ok, aim out there at that tank and fire", he ordered. "Sergeant I don't know how to fire it", came my reply. He turned me down range, put the LAW on my shoulder, showed me how to aim through the view finder, and said, "Now, just press the trigger on top of the tube, and it will fire". I looked through the sight, put my fingers over the top of the tube where the trigger was, and as I pressed down on the trigger, the tube went down with the press and sheww-boom, I hit the ground ten feet in front of us and could have killed us.

The officer in the tower began yelling," What the hell is the matter with you?" I wanted to tell him that he was what the matter with me was, but just decided to walk off the range and get out of there. DUH?

Ft. Lewis was a beautiful place located in the northern rain forest near Seattle. We had six weeks of infantry training there. Toward the end of the training, I had decided to go to airborne school. One of my drill sergeants talked me out of it. "McBain, you got some brains, don't go airborne", he said to me privately. "Why", I asked, "You're airborne"? "You got orders for Nam", he said, "that means you'll get assigned to an airborne outfit...they're gung ho and will get you killed", he replied. This was confusing me. Here was an airborne Vietnam combat veteran, who was trying to talk me out of going airborne.

He kept after me about it and finally managed to convince me not to go airborne. I then got orders for only a two week leave when most of the others got thirty days. I never could understand who decided who got what, but was angry about only getting two weeks. I went home for a two-week leave forgetting about jump school, and excited to see my folks and friends.

In the two weeks I was on leave I had a few things to do. First I sat down with my Dad and told him to use any money I sent home if he needed it, and discussed the death thing. Next I caught a military hop from Wright Patterson AFB to Andrews AFB in Washington DC to see my brother John who was recently back from Vietnam, and had just been married. He took me on the grand tour of DC in his new pride and joy, a brand new 1968 Dodge Super Bee he had bought when he returned from the Nam. This was my first time in Washington, and I was in awe of all of the places we went to that I had heard about all of my life. We discussed Vietnam along the way while we climbed all of the stairs of the Washington Monument, and then to the Lincoln Memorial. We went to Arlington Cemetery, and the Smithsonian Institute. Lastly we went to the Navy Department where his wife worked to say hi.

Once back in Dayton, I went with some friends up to Ohio State to see other friends in school there and found they had bought front row, center section seats to the Who Concert that night for myself, and my two best friends Rory and Raz who were both heading for Navy Basic Training. It was the best rock concert I had ever been to, and they played their entire new album, the Rock Opera Tommy.

On the night before leaving for Vietnam, I was having a nice dinner with my parents and trying to be positive for their sakes. There was a knock at the back door of the house, and out-side were three of my friends motioning to me to come out. "Dick, we want to get an airline ticket to Canada for you", one of them said. Now I appreciated the fact that they were thinking of getting me away from a war they didn't believe in and being concerned for my safety, but I was somewhat taken back.

"Guys", I said, "all of these years and you have never known me. Do you really think that I would desert from the army?" They could see my disappointment in them for what they were doing, and I could see they now felt bad about it. "Look, I am scared to death about what's coming, but I can't run away from my responsibility", I explained. Any way we hugged and they left, and I had to prepare for tomorrow.

My best friend, Rory Mays, drove me to the airport. When he picked me up at my parent's house, I remember looking up at the window as we backed down the driveway. There was my Mother trying to keep a smile for me as I saw the tears running down her face as she realized that she could no longer protect me. An hour later I boarded a plane for Seattle.

When I arrived at Sea-Tac Airport, I caught the military transport to Ft. Lewis's Overseas Replacement station. We noticed a big difference in treatment by other soldiers. During training, we had been yelled at, cussed out, and called names. Now it appeared we were one of the team, and treated respectfully, which felt pretty good.

We spent the day and night getting ready. We were taken to the supply depot and issued four sets of jungle fatigues, two pairs of jungle boots, six pairs of green socks, six green T-shirts, six green boxer shorts, booney-hats, and other paraphernalia for the Nam.

That night, we sat around the barracks talking about what we expected, playing poker, and just trying to keep our minds off of the war. Even with all of the joking, laughing, and trying to look cool, most of us felt the stress of where we were going and the dangers of combat.

The next day we got up early and walked to the mess hall for breakfast. We realized that this was perhaps the first time we had not been marched or even run to the mess hall. We ate hearty then headed back to get our gear and repot to the transport area.

We loaded up and took a transport to McCord Air Force Base, where we sat in the building waiting for our call. As we walked out to the plane we saw it was a Flying Tiger Lines aircraft, and I was surprised. I remembered as a kid building a model plane of a Flying Tiger P-40 Tomahawk fighter plane used against the Japanese by our guys in China, and I wasn't aware that they had an airline. We boarded the plane and headed for Vietnam.

We stopped in Alaska for refueling, and practically froze trying to get into the airport. They were working on the gates, so the plane had to park out on the tarmac and we had to deplane in jungle fatigues and run for the terminal in snow and below freezing temperatures. While inside the terminal, I was amazed to see a number of Eskimo's in their huge fur coats and mukluks. We made one other stop in Japan where we deplaned for a short time, then on to Vietnam. The realism of the ominous future for all of us was hitting home and many of us just got quiet and stared out of the window, or into space.

CHAPTER THREE

ARRIVING IN "THE NAM"

When we got to the Cam Rahn Bay airbase, I guess I was expecting to see very few people, and thought we would probably be running for a bunker. Instead it looked almost like a USA Air Force base with paved runways and tarmac's, and many Air force personnel all over the place. As we slowed down, an air force truck with a big sign on top that read, "FOLLOW ME", led the plane to the place we would be getting off.

There was a lot of activity going on, and it was a little disturbing when we saw flag-draped metal boxes being loaded into the back of a C-130 transport on their final journey home.

Arriving at Cam Rahn Bay's replacement center, we were lined up as a Sergeant called out names, and I was assigned with about twenty others to bunker guard duty at Cam Rahn Bay. They took us to a guard house with bunks, and told us we would be on detail starting that evening for a few days to a week. They told us to go and get some chow and report back when we were done.

A few of us headed out to the mess hall to eat. On the way, the guys who had been in combat could be easily picked out from the "rear" guys, due to very faded camouflage covers on their helmets, and really beaten up jungle boots where all of the polish and some of the leather was worn off. Most of these guys had put in their year, and were waiting to go home. Every time we passed some on the road, they would ask, "Hey man, what's your MOS?" (Job designation) I would answer, "Eleven Bravo", which meant infantry. What disturbed me the most was that every single one of them would then say nothing, but instead drop their head and quietly walk away. Now this was very unnerving, and I was already scared, not only about being infantry, but facing a whole year of war.

After reporting back we were given a briefing on what we would be doing on Bunker guard duty. They told us what we would be watching for, and what to do about it if we saw it. They said we were not to fire claymores or even our own weapons at things we saw without first calling it in to get orders on what to do. They said that whatever position we were assigned would be visited by the duty officer hourly, and he may instruct us to fire a pop-up flare now and again, or something else, but we were not to do it unless ordered to. They told us we would have an M-14 with one bullet and no more. I was appalled at how stupid that was, but hey, who was I?

One of the nights I was in a tower on the bunker line, and spotted movement to our front about one hundred meters out. As the man drew closer we called it in and immediately flares were sent up. This guy was running around yelling something that made no sense to me. He looked like a gook as he was shirtless with dark black hair, but he had on US jungle fatigue pants and boots.

Several men went out and brought him in under arms. As we questioned him, he was not making much sense. The MP's came and took him, and we later learned he was an AWOL soldier who had run off some six months ago and was living in a village with the Vietnamese. None of us could figure out why he would do that but he was back and now on his way to LBJ (Long Binh Jail), which was the in-country prison for deserters and other US soldier criminals.

One night in Cam Rahn Bay I was put on a road along the fence line, and given an M-14 with one round to guard the road. I felt incensed that they treated new guys like they were a danger, and wondered why they didn't consider the training we had already had. Unfortunately there were a few 'Dummies" in combat units and it was some of their actions that caused these ridiculous situations.

Anyway, out on that road in the dark and alone I felt a terrible urge coming on me to have to go to the latrine…I mean unbearable. My mind kept telling me that I couldn't leave my post for fear of court-martial, but my body told me to either go or have one heck of a mess in my fatigues. Well I ran off the road into the brush and did what I had to do, and fortunately was never caught, although the Officer of the Day came around to check on things very shortly after I returned to my post. I felt bad but was glad I had not been caught by minutes. It started to rain as the OD's jeep moved on and I of course became soaking wet, and it made me wonder how many times during a year in the jungle I would be soaking wet and uncomfortable. I later learned the answer…many!

Bunker guard at Cam Rahn Bay was not all bad. We worked shift hours, and during the day, we could go to the beach or into the town or just chill out. I figured that every day on guard was better than one in combat.

After a few days we fell out for orders and a Sergeant was there to assign individuals to different divisions. "McBain", yelled the Sergeant. "Here", I responded. "Hundred and First Airborne Division", he yelled back. The statement took me back. "Wait a minute Sergeant, I'm not airborne qualified", I yelled back in response. "You are now trooper", he smirked back at me, and continued on with the next name. I was in shock! How could this happen. I wanted the training to be airborne qualified, but was talked out of it. Now I was going into an airborne unit without the training; typical Army.

I boarded a C-130 and was flown to Bien Hoa AFB. From there I was taken for a little in-country training to the SERTS (Screaming Eagles Replacement Training School). There we were run through advanced jungle combat training, and some map and compass refresher courses that proved invaluable later on, as well as finding and dismantling booby traps, camouflage tactics, moving on-line in triple canopy jungle after contact with the enemy, and water conservation. One thing was for sure, that the 101st Airborne Division was keen on training, and as much as we all complained about it, many of us were thankful we had it when the stuff hit the fan.

We were then flown to Phu Bai AFB, very close to the Provincial Capital of Hue where one of the fierce battles of the 1968 Tet Offensive had been fought. From there we were loaded on a deuce and a half (2 ½ ton truck) and were transported to the base camp of the 101st Airborne Division, Camp Eagle which was not many miles away.

As we pulled into Camp Eagle, there was a large painted picture just inside the gate depicting a huge battle scene between the 101st and gooks. There was blood and explosions painted and then the caption that really caught my attention; "They've got us surrounded, the poor bastards". I began to remember what my Drill Sergeant had told me about airborne troops being very gung-ho, and this sign seemed to give his comments credence.

Company Sign at Camp Eagle

I was dropped off in front of a big sign that said "Strike Force", and was assigned to Co. A, 2nd Battalion, 502nd Infantry and went to check in at the orderly room. The Second Five O' Deuce became my home for my tour of duty, and I couldn't have served with a better group of men.

I went and drew my weapon and equipment from S-4, labeled my stateside duffel bag and turned it into them, then headed up to the chopper pad on a big hill near the Company area to be flown out to my company which was on Fire Support Base (FSB) Rifle.

As the "Slick" (Bell Huey UH-1) landed on the pad a few guys and I jumped on. This was the first of many rides on choppers I would experience. The doors were either open or not there at all, and I moved as close to the center as I could get for fear of falling out. Thomas, a point man for the company, was half hanging out of the door and I thought he was crazy.

As the chopper lifted off it soon felt like we were floating on air. It was a beautiful day and the warm air blowing through the chopper with the repetitive foop…foop…foop of the blades while we flew gave me a relaxing feeling. I always enjoyed flying in "Slicks" unless it was stormy or on our way to a hot AO. (Area of Operations).

Thomas asked where I lived to which I responded Dayton, Ohio. He was the first to call me "Cherry", a label given to new guys, and he talked a little about being a point-man and how good he was at it, and how I would have to get used to combat and living in the jungle. I looked out of the door as we flew over the triple canopy jungle trying to see any enemy and expecting I might. Rarely did we ever see any enemy when flying over the jungle as it is so thick and provides great cover.

The pilot turned to me and said we were coming into "Rifle". I looked out ahead and could see Firebase Rifle in the distance. It looked like a bald hill-top in the middle of thick jungle, and that's exactly what it turned out to be. As the chopper approached the landing pad, he pulled the front of the chopper up sharply to slow down our airspeed coming in, then just as fast leveled it out as he put it down softly on the pad. Many of these pilots amazed me at how they maneuvered the choppers to do all kinds of things, and they all seem to have their own style.

It was late November 1969 when we landed at FSB Rifle, and Thomas led me to the CP to report in. I was assigned to the second platoon, where I met Lt. Morehead, our platoon leader. After he briefed me on what to expect on the firebase, I remember him asking me, "McBain, what do you want out of your tour here?" I responded, "Sir I want two things; the first is to get out of here alive and the second is to make Five (E-5)". He said he expected I wouldn't have trouble getting either. LT. Morehead was great at keeping us on a positive track, which was a huge help in such scary times. LT. and his radio operator, Ed Matajesyk, had a little make-shift hooch set up with a small Christmas tree about two feet high, which was nice to see out in the middle of nowhere. He assigned me to the second squad and pointed out where they were on the firebase.

I next met Steve Clement who became my closest friend until he was killed. (Chapter One – Toss of a Coin) There were a few of the guys in second platoon that were labeled "Heads" by the others who were drinkers. The drinkers

My arrival to the company who were here on FSB Rifle - Steve Clement (standing) at left became my best friend until he was killed instead of me by a toss of a coin, detailed in Chapter One.

thought that the "heads" were somewhat loony due to the illegal nature of drugs, and the counter-culture going on in the world. Thomas, the guy I flew out with decided to tell the "heads" that I was a CID (Central Intelligence Division) agent undercover to locate drug users. Where he ever got that idea is beyond me, but as I later got to know the guys who were very cold to me at first, I found out there were one or two of them who were threatening to shoot me in a firefight if I was a CID agent.

One of the things I learned as time passed was that some of the guys would spout off with threatening words about killing this guy or that officer without ever meaning to do such. Our guys were all talk about those things but would never do it, as they were very proud, professional soldiers during their tours, and would no more kill Americans than their friends. We certainly heard the stories of "fragging" (using a fragmentation grenade) to kill this officer or that Sergeant, but they weren't in our unit.

They quickly realized I was no CID Agent, but were happy to label me "Cherry" for a while, a term all new guys had to bear until they thought differently. After being with the unit and in a couple of fire fights, I soon lost that title and fit right in.

Now Thomas had a side-kick we all called "Shorty". These two were good soldiers, but were like Mutt & Jeff as they were always arguing about minutia back and forth, and were quite funny to watch and listen to. When Thomas would say something Shorty considered outrageous, Shorty would simply reply, "Bull frog shit", and on they would go.

During the brief stay on FSB Rifle, we occupied our time filling sand bags, and laying concertina wire fences around the base, placing claymore mines, and setting trip flares. Most of the Fire Bases were "bald" hills surrounded by

Point-man Thomas and his sidekick "Shorty". They seemed to always be together yet argued like Mutt & Jeff. They were great friends anyway

triple canopy jungle, and it was eerie to be out in the open, so to speak, and realizing the enemy could be watching or even aiming at you from the thick brush where you couldn't see them.

Finally we were given orders to head out in the AO on a search and destroy mission, while another company would relieve us as FSB security. We were briefed and packed our stuff, and began our walk into the dark jungle. I found this first move for me into the uncut jungle for combat operations both exhilarating and scary as hell. I had no idea of what to expect but knew we had a purpose and that the enemy was in the area.

As I carried my rucksack loaded to the hilt in the jungle and with a radio on top of it, I realized how difficult humping these mountains was going to be. Then came my first hearing of combat operations on the radio, "Strike Force

Fiver this is Strike Force One – What is your sit-rep, over". The CO was establishing communication with the point squad. "Strike Force One this is Five, sit-rep negative, over", was the response. Sit-rep was code for situation report, and negative meant all was clear, so far.

The CO then asked all RTO's (Radio Telephone Operators) to do a "commo" check, and I was excited to call in my first words in combat. I called to the CO's RTO, "Strike Force One Alpha this is Strike Force Seven Alpha, commo check, how copy over". I was answered that I was heard loud and clear, and I was now on my way.

Moving was slow as our point squad was cutting through heavy brush and the CO wanted to move faster. Our CO then was a former Green Beret and a no nonsense man. He called forward and told them to get moving. I never noticed a change in speed and probably because the guys walking point weren't about to put themselves in unnecessary danger just because the CO, who was back toward the rear wanted to move faster. Every time the CO would call ahead and ask them what the holdup was, they would just acknowledge and ignore. In my opinion, they were the ones who were correct. We were under no time constraints and not headed to anything in particular, so why take chances.

We set up that evening in our NDP's (Night Defensive Perimeters) in our typical three man positions, and broke out the heat tabs to dry off and make coffee.
The first night out was a little nerve-racking for me, especially experiencing the complete darkness in the jungle; I couldn't see anything at all. The noises became

Dick's first squad on the side of an LZ at a machine gun position. Tom Brennan, Billy Lyman, Dick, "Caje" Faull, John Ridgeway, Bob Lawson, Willie Thomas

even more frightening as there was no way to tell what they were, but all of this soon became old-hat as time went on. After some time in the "Bush" we just crashed with creepy-crawlers and other critters running over us in the dark and rarely paid them any attention.

CHAPTER FOUR

CHRISTMAS OPERATIONS

Christmastime in Vietnam was very depressing. It was mid-monsoon season in the country, which meant rain most of the time. I spent Christmas in the jungle surrounding an LZ (Landing Zone) we had cleared on top of a hill. Along with our regular four-day resupply, we were getting hot turkey, dressing, and mail brought out to us. In the distance we heard the popping of chopper blades coming our way. As always, a yell came to "Pop smoke on the LZ". We always had to pop smoke grenades whenever a chopper was inbound. Any color but red meant it was OK to come in and land. Red smoke meant a "Hot LZ", which was one either non-secured or under fire.

Hot food was a treat for us, and everyone was scurrying to help set up and get their share. While we were eating, someone was distributing mail. "McBain" he called out. "Here" I said, and was surprised to get twenty-seven letters, which was my first mail catching up with me, and a goodies package from home. As I opened the package, I found Mom's wonderful Christmas cookies and was just sitting back against a tree to slowly savor some treats when, "Thump......Ka-boom", the sound of a grenade launcher and the subsequent explosion of the grenade shook me violently out of my ideas of resting. M-16's and AK-47's began rapid fire and I was scrambling with my weapon for cover.

When the firing stopped, we were all trying to find out what had happened. It turned out that two gook "trail-watchers" had seen our choppers leave, and they thought

Twenty-seven letters, the first mail that caught up to me, and a hot Christmas dinner on a LZ with a package from home with goodies in it went miles in making a demoralized, scared soldier happy again

we all had left, so they came up the trail to check out our buried trash for food. Unfortunately for them, out trail guards saw them first at let them have it; however in the excitement of the moment, they didn't hit them and began blaming each other for not getting them. Contrary to what some may believe, even the best shots can miss the enemy in these unexpected "taken by surprise" situations.

It was common for the enemy to check out our sites when they would see or hear us leave. Not only did we throw away many cans of c-rations we didn't like or want that they would gladly receive as food, but GI's were typically careless about other things the enemy could use. They could take used LAW's and create makeshift mortar tubes for their use. I know our unit always broke up the used LAW's so they couldn't.

It always amazed me of how they could Gerry-rig things left behind into weapons. They would take our c-ration cans, cut the bottoms out and use them for grenade booby-traps. They'd place a grenade in the open-ended can, attach a trip wire to the grenade, pull the pin as the can would hold the spoon intact, and place the trip wire so anyone hitting it would pull the grenade out of the can, throwing the spoon and killing the person. We always had to be aware of what we were leaving behind.

The jungle was a mixed bag of beauty and hardship. Triple canopy jungle is so thick that in many fire-fights you never saw the enemy you were firing at. We had to cut our way through much of it and were always seeing insects, snakes, and animals you don't see in the United States, with the exception of the zoo.

Although at night you many times couldn't see your hand in front of your face, the ground had some kind of phosphorescent coating on the twigs and leaves that sort of illuminated the ground in a greenish tint; it was very surreal! Once in a while we could see the sky through the trees and the stars, with obviously the same constellations we saw at home, which was always comforting to me.

"Good Lord, what in the hell is that", I said one day when we saw the most grotesque and scary looking insect I had ever seen. It was on the side of a tree trunk, and about the size of my fist with antennae, red eyes in an oddly shaped head, and a hard shell grey body. As I approached to get a better look, this thing let out a shrill noise that scared the heck out of me. We moved on!

Later I was on guard duty in our NDP, and usually we were in two or three man positions where one watched while the other two slept. We would change out usually every two hours. Keeping your watch could be very scary because

This is a depiction of what that scary bug looked like, but is not it. That insect lay quiet until I got too close then let out a loud freaky noise

you couldn't see anything, and when there was movement out in front of you, it could be the enemy or just an animal.

This particular night I had a strange happening. As I was looking out in front of me, not able to see a thing, I heard movement in the trees above me. I didn't know what to make of it as I thought "Charlie" would certainly not be in the trees above us. I already had my M-16 locked and loaded, and was aiming it at the noise when all of a sudden there was a crashing noise of branches and a large monkey actually fell out of the tree and landed what sounded like five feet in front of me. He started to scream in what sounded like a chimpanzee, but since I had never seen a chimpanzee where we were, I don't know what it was. It soon ran off leaving my heart still beating heavily, and I was very pleased to get off duty that night.

When I told what had happened the night before to a couple of my buddies they just nonchalantly said, "an der it is breeze". "Breeze" was the name we all called each other, taken from the common expression we used in the Nam, "Der it is Breeze". "Don't mean nothing", Willie chimed in, using another expression we used all of the time, that had multiple meanings, but usually meant, "No big deal, it doesn't matter"!

SSG's Hunter & Diaz on patrol and were both fine soldiers. SSG Diaz had previously been a pimp in New York City before entering the Army

Early the next morning we were told to quickly prepare to move out. "Saddle Up", Lt. Morehead said, "Move out", SSG. Hunter told Thomas our point man. In a couple of days we reached an area that was very eerie to move through. It was a large section of jungle that had been defoliated with Agent Orange. The tree trunks and brush were there, but all of the leaves had died and turned grey. It looked like the aftermath of a forest fire.

Agent Orange was a herbicide used by the United States to remove the cover of the jungle from suspected enemy strongholds. It certainly did the trick, but was later discovered to have caused many deaths and birth defects, and greatly affected Vietnam Vets who returned, and their families. We didn't know it at the time, but were told later

Sgt. Ray Neiman setting up his NDP (Night Defensive Position) in an Agent Orange defoliated area. We had no idea of the danger of Agent Orange at the time, but many of us found out much later

that Agent Orange, even though dry when we were in the defoliated areas, could get into our systems by breathing the dust in the air. I never thought much about it while in the jungle and saw that it certainly opened up these areas so our aircraft could spot and kill the enemy much easier. We ran into Agent Orange areas of the jungle on a number of occasions, but never gave a thought that it might hurt us.

We were operating in platoon strength in three different directions. We were "humping" 60 - 80 lbs. rucksacks not including the extra water and radio I had, up and down small mountains all week. As my squad was walking point moving in a thick jungle area down the side of a mountain, we reached the base of the ravine before we realized we had walked into a bunker complex dug into the narrow area between two mountains. Both sides of the ravine raised up about six hundred feet, with the ravine measuring one hundred feet across at the bottom, and nearly two hundred

On patrol we walked into this bunker complex, most of which were usually hard to see until you were on top of them. Caje covers an entrance with his M-60 machine gun, while others spread out watching for other escape routes

yards at the top. LT got to his radio operator who had the CP on "push", and called in for artillery and air strikes. We quickly climbed back up the side of the mountain we had just descended, returning the light small arms fire coming from some of the bunkers. After adjusting the artillery coming in, LT was putting a lot of 155, HE rounds (Highly Explosive) right on top of the sighted bunkers in an attempt to keep the enemy pinned down until the jets arrived.

The setting was like a stadium, with us in the "high" seats. We sat along the ridge of the mountain as the two F-4 Phantom Jets came on push. "Puddles 25 this is Nightmare One, cancel artillery, and mark the target for us...over", came the voice of the lead pilot. LT acknowledged, and called for us to get to a position to throw smoke grenades to mark the target. What none of us saw was the movement of two gooks with a 51 caliber machine gun moving up the other side of the ravine, and setting up on a ridge to shoot at the planes.

F4 Phantom Jet coming in to make his run on the bunker complex with his wingman following. These planes helped and even saved us many times with close-in bombing

The first Phantom rolled in to mark the target with a "Willie Peter" (white phosphorous) rocket, so we could confirm he had the right spot. As he came in to the narrow gap between the two mountainsides over the ravine, I remember his cockpit was level with where we were sitting.

He looked over at us as he flew by, and it seemed we could almost reach out and touch him.

Just then, the gook machine gun opened up from the other side, and tracers were directing them to the Phantom. The pilot quickly rolled out and up to the right, and we heard him tell his other pilot to pull out of his target run.

"That son of a gun is shooting at me", the first pilot said almost jokingly. "Watch this", he said as he went into a steep climb, doing a flip-over, and heading back to the point of contact. The two enemy gunners were firing frantically at the diving jet coming right toward them. The pilot, right in front of us at eye level again, released a 500 pound bomb that appeared like it was released far too early, and pulled out into another steep climb. We watched as the bomb headed right for the enemy machine gun, and exploded right on top of them, blowing the whole ridge line off of the side of the mountain, with trees, bodies, and dirt flying some 40 feet into the air in front of us. "That'll teach 'em", the pilot replied.

He and his wingman then both rolled into about four more dives on the bunker complex, completely destroying anything that had been there. "Thank you Nightmare", LT said as they were flying over to assess their strike. "Roger Puddles", said the pilot, "call us anytime…happy to oblige, out", he said as they departed. We watched the two jets go off until we couldn't see them anymore, and all sat and talked about what great and accurate pilots we had in the Navy and Air Force.

We started out again, walking down the mountainside to make sure that the bunkers were completely destroyed. The Phantom's had done a great job on the bunkers, which were now nothing but gaping holes in the ground. We briefly looked around to see if the explosions has revealed anything we didn't see earlier, but everything was covered by dirt from the explosions.

We humped another click (1000 meters) or so, looking for a place to set up for the night. As we climbed down a ridge to a flat place in the mountain, a "Cherry" saw a large Bengal tiger and fired at it with his M-16. Unfortunately he hit the big cat, but only wounded him. The distance we were from the tiger was far more than anyone should have taken a shot from, and our LT was really ticked off about it, and for good reason. He had wounded the Tiger and there was no way to tell how badly; we found out soon enough!

That night was one of the most nerve-racking ordeals I remember. No one was able to sleep because the wounded tiger circled us all night, crashing through the jungle and roaring about 25 meters in front of our night perimeter positions. We were just waiting for that 200-pound monster to come running in to grab one of us. Imagine pitch dark jungle and all we could depend on was our hearing. It seemed like it might have gone away a few times then suddenly "grrrrrowwww" which made it sound like it was right in front of you, and maybe it was.

I worked for a retired Sergeant First Class just before I went into the Army who had recently returned from Vietnam. He told me of a time a small group of his men were surrounded in close proximity at night in the jungle, and a tiger attacked one of the men and started dragging him away by the shoulder. He said they couldn't shoot because it would give their position away, but one of the men managed to use his large knife to kill the tiger. I had never forgotten that story and he swore it was true, and now it was easy to see he wasn't kidding.

The fear lasted all night, and finally ended just before daybreak when the growling stopped. It turns out that the tiger had finally bled to death, and was found by a couple of the guys when they went out to retrieve their claymore mines. Unfortunately, the damage had been done and it seemed we were all on edge due to no sleep and being extremely nervous all night.

It's amazing how tight you get in such a short time with the guys in your squad and platoon. Since we usually operated in platoon strength, those are obviously the guys you get to know and trust the best. When the shooting starts you know you're not alone, but your close buddies are right there with you, watching out for one another by operating as a team.

When out on patrol, if we walked into an ambush or surprised the enemy and a firefight ensued, we knew our brothers were on their way to help. As soon as we heard firing, radio contact was made for the location and LT would send a squad or two to get them out. Our guys were so well trained in laying out a proper base of fire and moving on line, that most of the time the enemy was killed or di di mau'd out of the area before we'd get there.

It was time for our four-day re-supply again, and we humped until we found a suitable hilltop on which to clear an LZ. We called for the usual "Kick-out" of axes, dynamite, and other various tools needed to clear the jungle from the top of the hill.

The squads got busy cutting down the small trees, and clearing the brush. Each squad had a "demo-expert" who had been trained to use explosives to remove the big trees, and rocks. I was the appointed "demo" man for my squad, and several of us were detailed to take dynamite to the base of the mountain to blow a huge tree that was in the way of a clear aircraft entry.

We took a whole case of dynamite with us down the mountainside, not knowing how much we would need. Once we found the base of the tree, it was so large that three men couldn't encompass it with arms outstretched. After some discussion, we all decided that no one was sure how much TNT it would take to blow the tree, and we didn't want to carry the extra weight of the remaining dynamite back up the mountainside, so we strapped the whole case to the tree.

The tree was probably one hundred and fifty feet high, with a very straight trunk that protruded about fifteen feet above the top of the mountain. We ran electrical cord back up over the mountain, and hooked it to a firing device. "Pop red smoke…pop red smoke", we shouted. After the smoke was in the air we yelled the blasting warning, "Fire in the hole….fire in the hole…fire in the hole". As the men took cover, the firing device was activated. "Ka-boooom", went the blast that shook the whole hill. What we saw next was quite incredible. The tree "Lifted-off" like a rocket. It started slowly at first, and then very quickly lifted straight up into the air. As it cleared the top of the "hill", it just exploded, splintering huge hunks of wood everywhere. They were falling all around us, and I knew we had just really screwed up. After making sure no one has injured, we started back down the mountainside. We were trying to hide from the Company Commander, who was by then yelling obscenities and trying to find us. Thank God no one was hurt, and the CO forgave us after he cooled down. That was my last attempt in rocketry.

Resupply in the Boonies was usually a happy time. More food, mail, ammunition and cigarettes including toiletries like razors, shaving cream, and then of course, candy

The hill was then clear for the resupply to be brought in and a few choppers arrived. One by one we emptied out the cases of c-rations, soft-drinks, mail bags, and whatever. We then loaded back on the axes and saws that they had kicked out earlier to use to clear the top of the ridgeline.

Other than the Squad guarding the LZ, every one pitched in to offload the choppers that came in with the resupply, and to insure anything they ordered from S-4 got to them and not to others, like a jungle sweater. During the monsoon everyone wanted one to keep warmer at night. Unfortunately, if you weren't right there to get it when it came in, someone else would take it as so many were ordered but they trickled in and weren't labeled.

Resupply was always looked forward to since it brought the usual things we needed, and every once in a great while some beer. We divided the stuff up, which was quite a task as it seemed everyone who smoked wanted the menthol cigarettes. In the typical sundries box that came with every resupply, there were usually only a few cartons of the menthol cigarettes, Salem's and Kool's. Tropical Hershey bars which were made not to melt, but many times had a white film on them from whatever they used to accomplish the non-melting, along with razors, toothpaste and the like all were in these boxes too. They usually brought out a few cases of soft-drinks, but many times instead of Cokes and Pepsi's it was Fresca; uughhh! Another huge treat with resupply that came very rarely were LRRP's (Long Range Recon Platoon) freeze dried meals you just added hot water to, and they were great compared to C-rations.

Some days later, we were extracted by choppers, and taken to another LZ somewhere out in another AO. In Northern I-Corps where we had our combat operations, it was either extremely hot or extremely wet. In the hot season we were always wet from sweat, and I mean soaked. Most of us always had a green towel around our necks to continually wipe off our faces. Heat exhaustion would hit someone periodically, and rarely a heat stroke happened, but the medics were diligent to see that we had the necessary salt pills to replenish body salt lost from profuse sweating.

Our unit carried a four day resupply which made one large rucksack for each of us. Humping those rucksacks up and down that mountainous terrain covered in thick jungle in 110 plus heat could wear out the strongest men very quickly. Water was crucial to carry on and stay alive in such heat, and many of us added to the weight of our rucksacks by clipping on extra canteens during the hot season.

In the monsoon season we were always soaked from rain; beaucoup rain. The monsoon in our part of the country ran from mid-October to late March or early April. During those approximate six months we would be wet all day if we were "humping the boonies", and looked forward to setting up for night where we could build a hooch with two poncho's buttoned together and get dry. We could not have

Heat tab stove with canteen cup on it. Also a pineapple jam can and hot chocolate pack from C-rations

fires in the jungle as it would give our position away, so we had to make a little "stove" out of a shallow C-ration can. We made these by using a can opener to punch holes in the can that would vent the heat tabs we used to heat our food, water for coffee, and get our clothes dry.

After setting up our poncho hooch's we would get under them and use a heat tab in the can stove and put our poncho liner around us and the stove to let the heat dry our clothes. Sometimes a guy would put his head under the poncho liner but he'd be out soon as the heat tabs gave off a noxious odor that would burn your eyes terribly.

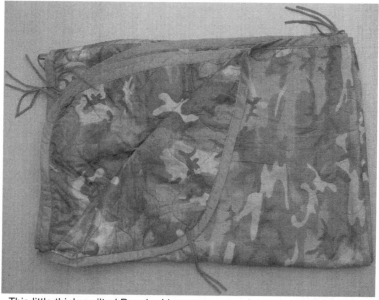

This little thinly quilted Poncho Liner was as much to a jungle fighter as a coat in winter. There were no sleeping bags or fires, and your poncho liner was what you had to sleep in and wrap up in to keep warm in the monsoon season. It also helped to keep mosquitoes off of you anytime

In addition to drying our jungle fatigues, this process would also dry our poncho liner, which is what we wrapped around us to sleep in. We didn't have sleeping bags but were given these poncho liners, which were camouflaged thin nylon quilts. These were precious to us for warmth at night in the monsoon season, and still used in the hot season to keep the mosquitoes off of us.

Mosquitoes were large in the jungle, and the anopheles mosquito spread malaria. Most soldiers faithfully took their anti-malaria pills; those who didn't many times caught the disease.

Unfortunately the poncho hooch's didn't always work. There were nights when I would be lying on my back, rolled up in my poncho liner and sound asleep. At first I would be thinking I was having a bad dream, but quickly woke up and realized it was real. The poncho on the ground snapped to the other poncho over our heads was letting a stream of water in that was running right down my back. It was extremely uncomfortable.

Getting up to fix it while being wet and cold again was even worse. I would have to feel around in the dark, not being able to see anything, and find the place that water was coming in. Then depending on the terrain we were laying in, I would attempt to get up and go out back in the rain and readjust the poncho material. The attempt was to raise the bottom poncho up above the stream of water running down the hill we were on, so it would go under the poncho and not through it. Of course sometimes I was so tired I would just let it flow and try to move to the right or left of it which never really worked, leaving nice cool water running down my back until my next watch.

There were also times that because of exhaustion we would just wrap up in our poncho liners, then wrap around us the outer-poncho, and just plop down in the mud and go to sleep. Thinking about that now astonishes me wondering how we could have done that. The answer was exhaustion from humping all day, and of course our youth, making all of that possible.

Another danger of the monsoon season was that it made it easier for "Charlie" (Viet Cong) to sneak up on us as the sound of the rain on all of the jungle brush made it hard to hear anything but the rain. Being awakened by your buddy for your turn at guard duty while it was raining was a real

Dick next to poncho hooch made from at least two ponchos clipped together and tied off at the corners to sleep under when raining. This was the best shelter we had in the jungle, and didn't always keep the water off of us

pain. You had finally managed to get to sleep and warm, and now it was out in the rain in pitch dark for two hours, and being able to hear nothing but the rain on all the jungle brush, and seeing nothing but black. At night, due to the complete darkness in triple canopy jungle, you had to rely on your hearing for security, and with the rain most that was taken away. What was left was your dependence on your trip-flare placement, and a hope that you had camouflaged them well enough where "Chuck" couldn't find them.

Once in a while during the day in the monsoon season, the sun would come out and do a lot to lift our spirits. One advantage we did take with all of the rain was stripping down and taking a bar of soap to have an outside shower. We tried to wash whenever the opportunity arose. Afterward, if you were lucky enough to have finally received a jungle sweater, you would put it on while the others wondered how you got yours. Also, you'd better make sure it was kept in the bottom of your ruck, or it was likely to disappear.

CHAPTER FIVE

COMBINED OPERATION WITH AVRN'S

In late February we were moved to a remote area to participate in a joint operation with the ARVN's (Army Republic of Viet Nam). Each American soldier was teamed with two ARVN's, and placed in a cordon around a village suspected of VC (Viet Cong) activity.

The village we cordoned was a small farming village surrounded by rice paddies. This was my first time of only a few that we operated in and around rice paddies. We normally were inserted by helicopter into the mountainous regions covered by thick jungle, but this was a place out of the mountains.

As we moved at night to find our positions, I remember how I tried to stay on the dyke tops as we walked, but managed to get my feet wet in the paddies once or twice. Once we surrounded the village we took up positions that insured we had no gaps of coverage.

My position was on a dike in a rice field outside of the village. I took the first watch, and told the ARVN's, "You two take the second watch together, and make sure to keep each other from falling asleep". I don't think they had a clue what I was saying, but I hoped that my gestures would tell the story.

Sitting on the dike that night I began to realize what a blessed life I had where I had grown up. I had always lived in a nice house, in a clean and comfortable middle class neighborhood, where doing chores around the house was to keep things up. These people worked their butts off day and night just to survive. Thy lived on the rice they grew, and lived in shacks with grass roofs and no electricity, sanitation, or even water on hand unless there was a well. Being in South Vietnam they had to worry not only about physical survival, but also about the Viet Cong who used southern villagers to store weapons and food, and treated them cruelly.

When I woke them up for their watch, I reminded them to keep awake while I slept, and to "Wake me in two hours" motioning to my watch the holding up two fingers. They mumble something like, "Yea, yea, ok Joe" but I didn't feel assured. I was anything but comfortable trying to sleep while these two took the watch, but I had no choice.

I was a very light sleeper during the war, and woke up after about forty-five minutes of sleep. As I sat up on the dike, I looked around in the dark, and found no sign of the two ARVN's. They had left me asleep by myself while they decided to go into the village and visit the local pleasure house. They were lucky they didn't come back. I always felt that the ARVN's were next to worthless, and this did little to disprove that notion.

The next day, I was moved to a gate of the village to check people going in and out. Our orders were to check the papers of anyone coming out to make sure they weren't the enemy. If things seemed out of place we were instructed to get them to the CP for interrogation.

As usual, the kids of the village would come out and ask for anything they thought we would give them. We also had to be careful as they were experts in stealing. They didn't "pick-pocket" anything, they would gather around you and several would grab your hands like they were playing. Once they had your attention, another one or two would move behind you and use a razor blade to quickly and silently slice the edge of your pocket and remove your wallet. Those kids would be long gone before you discovered it. I never got over how those cute little, and I

Dick McBain with the village kids in a combined cordon operation with the ARVN's (Army Republic of Vietnam). Dick is feeding the kids his C-rations at his checkpoint where they came out to meet him

mean little kids, were so adept at stealing, and manipulating your feelings to get what they wanted. I guess if I were used to struggling just to survive, especially with a war going on around me in my backyard, I would have been clever and calculating also.

I was fortunate enough to learn what to do to protect my wallet by seeing others having things stolen by the kids in villages, and always kept my wallet in my breast pocket buttoned down and watching every move. Whenever we came upon villages in the jungle, which was not too often, the kids would come out to sell stuff. You could buy a pack of neatly rolled marijuana "Joints" for ten dollars if you wanted, and of course we always had the privilege of buying our own Cokes and Pepsi's back for five dollars each.

What would happen was that the gooks would attack the supply trains in the lowlands, and steal most of the Cokes and Pepsi's off of them. Then they would sell them to GI's when they came near. Unfortunately, they would leave the Fresca, and many times that was all we would get on resupply. Most of us disliked Fresca, and would get ticked off when that is all we would get. There was a time or two when we stacked the Fresca and fired it up in protest. Of course these were protests no one but us ever saw. Such was life in the land of the Nam.

The kids were always cute and friendly and used that to take advantage of us. They knew many of us GI's would give food, candy, c-rations, and pretty much whatever we had because we felt compassion for their situation. They also wanted cigarettes which seemed strange for such young kids. I turned around for a second and saw a little two or three year old boy lighting up a cigarette he found in my rucksack. I was astounded. I looked at what may have been his older brother to have him take it, but he just past it off with the wave of his hand as no big deal.

After giving all of my C-rations to the kids who were obviously hungry, I encountered a man coming out of the

Dick shared some cigarettes with one of the kid's father's. He then handed one to each of the two little kids walking around and they started smoking. I couldn't believe my eyes

village who looked suspicious. I asked him for his papers, and they were not in order. I pointed my M-16 at his face and said, "You VC"! He pleadingly denied it, and my interpreter told me that he claimed to be PF (Popular Forces), who were local's fighting for the south as we were. I decided I had to take him in for interrogation, and started on the long walk through rice paddies to the command post.

I had the suspected enemy walk about twenty feet in front of me, while I kept my rifle on him. In passing several checkpoints some of the guys would say, "Hey Mac, the CP is quite a ways away. Just shoot him and save yourself the walk". Now I must point out that even though this was said a few times, no one meant it. They were just passing the time with bad jokes. I never saw anyone killed by our guys in cold blood, and was distressed to hear of the My Lai massacre a year before. I was with a very gung ho outfit, but in my experience we would go out of our way, even to the point of risking our own lives to make sure that innocent civilians weren't hurt.

As we were crossing a third rice paddy, a large bull water buffalo, the beast of burden for the farmers, turned toward me and let out a loud grunt. I thought, Oh no, not this too. Sure enough, the bull put his head down getting ready to charge me, and I just stood there ankle deep in rice paddy water, trying to decide what I would do. The bulls didn't care much for strangers in uniform, and caused a real

Water Buffalo – their beast of burden – didn't like Dick and charged him. The potential enemy he was taking in for interrogation jumped in front of him and stopped the bull

dilemma for us when these situations would happen. If I were to shoot the beast, I would be fined five hundred dollars, according to policy; and if I didn't, I could be trampled by this large bull, and buried in the middle of this rice paddy.

The bull started his run toward me. He was about thirty-five yards away when I brought my weapon up to shoot him. Just then, the suspect I was taking in jumped in front of me, and rattled off some Vietnamese. The bull stopped dead, turned around and walked away. The suspect smiled at me, and I felt like a jerk.

When we arrived at the command post, I waited outside to see what they would find out about this guy who just saved me from either being trampled, or fined five hundred dollars. It turned out he was with us, and his papers were wrong because he was a spy for us. He had been in the village gathering intelligence for this operation when he was found out. He fled hastily out of the village through my gate with papers designed to show he was VC. He came out before I left, and I thanked him for stopping the bull.

Later that day the operation was finished, and I heard it had been a success. I never heard a shot fired so there must have been some intelligence gathered, but nothing else happened at my position with the exception of the kids selling us back our own stuff.

We were extracted by helicopter, and taken to a fire base on a hill overlooking the South China Sea. We remained there for a week or so securing the artillery company who were in support of our battalion. While there I managed to drink some contaminated water, and was hospitalized for a week with dysentery. I lost twenty pounds, and was running out back of the hospital to the "crapper" as we called it, about thirty times a day. Man was I sore. I returned to the firebase a week later still feeling pretty drained.

While pulling guard duty at the firebase, we would periodically fire tracers over sampans (small fishing boats) that would come close to shore. Many times these were manned by Viet Cong to make surveillance on the positions of the artillery pieces, so we couldn't let them get too close.

Firebase duty was pretty much an eight hour day doing guard duty on the perimeter, repairing wire fences, taking care of jungle-rot and leach bites from the jungle, going on patrols in and around the firebase, and if you were unlucky, burning crap from the latrines. In the jungle we were pretty much on duty, or at least on alert 24/7, and the firebase duty gave us some needed rest during our off duty hours. When off duty we would play cards, usually poker, or pal around with the guys. Some of us would play guitars, and I learned to play on firebase duty, while others would improve their sleeping hooch's with more sandbags and pieces of metal for the roofs.

One night a few of us were off duty sitting on the edge of the hill that the fire base was on, just listening to tapes, and staring into the jungle in front of us. There was a joint being passed around and all of us were beginning to feel melancholy. "Wow, man, how can it seem so peaceful in the middle of a war", asked Bishop as the music played. Dig it man, what the hell are we doing here anyway, someone else chimed in. The world seems in turmoil, the country seems against us, and all we're doing is trying to survive and do our duty, yet here, tonight, on the top of this hill all seems peaceful.

Well as the situation had it, the statement about peaceful was soon corrected. As the music played on, we saw a firefight break out across the lagoon to our right front. We could see both American and enemy tracers that were firing at each other. It was very dark outside, and we were high up on a hill. The firefight was so far away that we barely could hear the guns fire, but we saw the red (American)

Doc Shenk, Blondie, Muff, Larry & Mel on the FSB. Some of the guys would fire our hand-held pop-up flares at the little boats that would slowly creep their way toward us in the lagoon below as a warning

and green (NVA) tracers in massive numbers going at each other.

While this was happening, the radio was playing, "C'mon people now, smile on your brothers, everybody get together, try to love one another right now", a familiar Jessie Collin Young and the Youngblood's song back in the world. It was surreal!

CHAPTER SIX

STAND-DOWN?

The SOP (Standard Operational Procedures) of the Second Five O' Deuce was to go out on operations for 60- 90 days at a time, which included both combat operations and rotating with other companies of the Battalion to secure our artillery at various firebases. At the end of those 90 days we were to get a two day stand-down in the rear for rest and different forms of debauchery. In my year it seemed we rarely got the two day's rest.

Combat extraction – as the choppers came in, the next group would run and jump on as the "Bird" pulled out and the next came in, and so on until all were picked up. Then we were taken to the next AO

First we would be extracted by chopper from the AO, and usually brought to FSB Bastogne, which was a large fire support base a few miles out from Camp Eagle. From there we would be picked up by deuce and a half's and taken the rest of the way into our base camp. We would be looking forward to getting clean clothes, a shower, and some rest time, but also would talk about what we would be facing as far as training and other duties.

As we arrived at Eagle, the rear guys would all come out on the landings of their hooch's, and always looked in awe of the airborne infantry coming in from combat. They would point at us, wave, and make comments to themselves about these bad-ass dudes coming in. We would usually be filthy, carrying all kinds of weapons, and camouflage junk hanging on some of us, and I guess we did look the part. We played it down to ourselves, but it did make us feel unique and special.

Command Sargent Major Walter J. Sabalauski, our Battalion CSM was a hard nose guy, but highly decorated from several wars and well respected

Of course, the trucks no sooner stopped in our battalion

area when we would see Command Sergeant Major Sabalauski waiting for us. He was a short, stocky, bald-headed polish man who acted mean and indifferent to anyone else except the Battalion Commander. Once in a while he would come out into the boonies to see us, and then he was entirely different, almost one of the guys so to speak. Unfortunately in the rear base camp he was a tough, snide, ornery old guy that acted like he would beat his own brother if he looked at him crossways.

"Fall-in" he would shout to us in what sounded like a critical and somewhat ashamed tone. He wasn't the least bit impressed like the other rear guys, because he had been in WWII and Korea, and very decorated but could be a real pain in the butt.

Command Sergeant Major Sabalauski's awards include the Distinguished Service Cross, Silver Star, Legion of Merit, 8 Bronze Stars, 3 Air Medals, 6 Army Commendation Medals, 4 Purple Hearts, 3 Awards of the Combat Infantryman's Badge, and the Master Parachutist Badge along with campaign medals for service in World War II, Korea, Dominican Republic, and Vietnam. He was so highly decorated that we all respected him but didn't like his manner very much.

"Get a haircut", he would yell as one of his first statements, "and get a shower and clean uniforms" he continued. "You men are 101st Airborne and you'd better start looking like it. Any one not clean shaven will get extra duty" he would continue, "and get those grenades taped up. Now move out and don't let me see you until it's all done!"

Grenades had to be wrapped with tape when in the rear if we had some, to secure the spoons from accidently flying as some of them were pretty beaten up. We usually had to turn in our rifles, claymores, LAW's and any other ordinance we would be carrying. I never liked it when we had to turn in our weapons as we got used to always having them by our sides in case of enemy attack. However, there were times at night when men would get very drunk while on stand-down, and get in fights where a squad from one platoon would get in a stupid argument against a squad of another platoon about who was better at this or that. Drunks never make much sense, and don't think well enough to have weapons around.

The Sergeant Major was not a favorite of mine as I saw no need for immediate harassment the minute we got in, but that was his nature. He was as hard on the Lieutenants as he was on us, and even though they technically out-ranked him, they didn't dare speak up.

The problem with being in the rear area base camp is that the higher-ups feel the need to keep everyone busy or occupied in some way, at least during the day. If we came in on a stand-down and did not have training lined up to keep us busy, the First Sergeant would pick details to do what the Vietnamese civilians ordinarily did when we were in the bush.

One of the favorites of all details was crap-burning. The latrines in Vietnam were not over dug out pits like the old outhouses. These were wooden buildings with a fifty gallon drum cut off leaving about two feet of the drum under the toilet seats. There were access doors in the rear of the building where the container would be drug out away from the building and then the contents set on fire. This was accomplished by us pouring diesel fuel into the container, lighting it, and then periodically stirring it to keep it burning. This was of course a dirty, smelly job and would take quite some time for each container to burn up the contents: sometimes hours. This was usually a "Cherry" detail where the new guys were taught the finer things in life in a war zone. If some old timer did something wrong or pissed a Sergeant off, he may be assigned to help them. I only remember doing this a couple of times when I was new, but it was a lousy detail to be on.

When I first got to the company area I had to go to the latrine. There was a big one with probably twelve seats in it (six to a side), and these big ones were wood siding about half way up, then screened the rest of the way with the roof hanging over. I went into this open latrine and there was a female Vietnamese civilian in there mopping the wooden floor. She just smiled at me and I told her to leave. She let me know in no uncertain terms in rattled off Vietnamese language that she was cleaning. I then told her to get out. She went out muttering under her breath.

As I sat down on one of the seats, and was sitting there about three minutes when in walks another female Vietnamese and pulls up her skirt and sits right down next to me to do her business. She just looked up at me like this was an everyday event, nodded her head and finished. She was in and out in two or three minutes then gone, but this was something I didn't like at all. From that day on I would go and use the single seat Officers' Latrine right behind the orderly room. I was always afraid of being caught, but never was. Of course we weren't in the rear area very often, and I often went at night when most were asleep.

Sometimes on a stand-down, which was supposed to be our break, some of the guys would be put on bunker guard at night around the base camp perimeter. On an occasion during the day, one of the guys would go into a town nearby and get some Obenzedrine which we called "Oscar Bravo". This was a legal amphetamine in the Nam, and it came in a bottle containing green syrup that was poured into cokes, and users would be up and wired all night.

"Oscar Bravo" was a heavy "speed" amphetamine and anyone using it would talk non-top, and fast. These guys where funny to see by someone not "speeding", however it would drive those around them nuts in short order. Users would be coming down in the morning and were all ready to crash and get some sleep. They just hoped there was no training or something that would not allow them to rest, but

Dick and Lt. Morehead just in for a stand-down, standing behind their orderly room at Camp Eagle. Dick still had on dirty jungle fatigues with his knife on his leg, beer in hand, and pockets full of who knows what

usually if there was they would still be given off for being on guard all night. Stand-downs were great for drinking some beer, catching up on mail, seeing a Korean Band show or movie in the company area, and just relaxing.

This particular stand-down was one where I wanted to catch up on my correspondence, and listen to a tape from home that I had been carrying around until we got to the rear where I could borrow a tape player. After that I would then see what mischief I could get into, but unfortunately the mischief would come first and the rest would have to wait until later.

I was just sitting down to hook up a tape machine when I looked up and here they came. "Mac, it's time to get drunk", was chimed together by both Doc Shenk and SSG. Johnson. We had become drinking buddies whenever we got into the rear, and they had been looking for me since we got cleaned up. I have to admit that I was hiding from them so I could get done what I wanted before they found me, knowing they would be looking for me to start tying one on.

"Aw common you guys let me get a couple of things done first and I'll find you", I pleaded. "No way Mac, we're going to get relaxed right now", SSG. Johnson said while Doc took my tape recorder away from me. "Ok, Ok, but I need to put this in a safe place because I borrowed it", I responded.

After I stashed the tape recorder in a safe place, we headed up to the Enlisted Man's Club, which was just a small hooch containing a bar and a couple of dozen tables. After a short wait we got our table and began the ritual of unhindered beer drinking. As usual, we all got wasted, and our excuse was that only in the rear did we see enough beer to get loaded with.

Later that evening we had another thing we looked forward to on stand-down's, which were the shows they would set up for us. There was a make-shift stage in the battalion area and they would usually have a Korean band with girls in it to do a show. They played mostly popular songs from the USA, and they were pretty good musicians. Of course the

Stand-downs were to give a well-deserved break to combat troops. One of the main attractions was Korean band's the Army would bring in for entertainment. The short skirted girls were a big attraction

guys were more interested in watching the girls, but the shows were a very nice break in getting our mind-set out of the war for a few hours.

The next day one of my friends and I ventured outside Camp Eagle to the town to see what they had there. We walked around and I must admit I was a little nervous, as we had all turned in our weapons. We went into some of the shops and I was amazed at some of the junk they sold there. On the other hand, the junk was mixed in with some real quality stuff.

Walking down the street my buddy asked me if I wanted to get a massage. I quickly told him no thanks as I had told myself I was not going to do any sex thing while in Vietnam. I was single and had no girlfriend at home, but I wanted to stay as close to the Lord as I could in this war zone. My friend assured me this was a legitimate massage parlor with no sex, and I agreed to go. I had never in my life had a massage, so this was going to be another first for me.

We went in and he and I were taken to the same room, and were told to take our clothes off and wrap our lower section in the large towels they gave us. Two girls came in wearing short-shorts and blouses and told us to get on the table face down. I became nervous and uncomfortable because I had no idea what to expect, and I was now facing away from this Vietnamese girl, something I never made a habit of doing.

She began with the oil rubdown on backs and legs which I'll admit felt very good. Then there was a slight pause before I realized she had climbed up on the table and then stood on my back. I jumped up quickly thinking she was going to try and break my neck or something, and almost threw her on the floor.

She shouted some Vietnamese at me and my friend, who had obviously done this before, told me to relax. "Dick, it's part of the massage. They walk up and back on your spine and it feels good, believe me", he said. I agreed and although I was edgy, I admit it felt good. They did our chest and legs when we turned over, and we got clothed, paid them, and left. I had been expecting something else with all that I had heard about massage parlors, but this one was straight, and I was then glad for the experience.

That night they had a movie that had just been released in the States. We hadn't heard of it yet, but it was a treat. It was MASH with Donald Sutherlin and Elliot Gould, and we found it quite funny. On the other hand our officers did not find it funny at all being that it made officers look like comical goof-offs breaking all of the rules.

After the movie, our Company XO came up to me and said, "McBain, you can't possibly think that was funny". Now I liked and respected this Airborne Ranger First Lieutenant, but he needed to loosen up so I just said, "Oh common LT, lighten up, it's a comedy". I should have left it there but just had to go on and say, "And I think it depicted most officers in the Army". Now I was just kidding but it really pissed him off. He just stormed off shaking his head and mumbling under his breath.

Another treat was the hot food we got on stand-down which we rarely got in the boonies except for holidays if they could get to us. We many times grilled our own steaks and hamburgers that the First Sergeant would get for us when they knew we were coming in to the rear. Just the hanging out and having a couple of days to do what we wanted, at least when we weren't training, went a long way in resting us and bringing some fun back in.

The day following our arrival, we found out that this was a working stand-down. Early the next morning, with most of us still trying to sober up, we were assembled and trucked out to a training ground where we saw a 60 ft. high tower. Our CO told us we were going to receive rappelling and slack-jump training that day.

There was no more parachuting for the 101st in Vietnam due to the triple canopy jungle making it near impossible. However, there were times certain units would need to slack-jump into a combat situation, and we all needed to be trained to do it. Rappelling was necessary to know also, because there were times in the mountains someone would fall or lose a piece of equipment that could only be recovered by this method.

After a class in making a "Swiss-seat" rope harness and use of the D-ring, we lined up to climb the tower. The first thing we had to do is rappel down the wooded side of the tower. I got hooked up and backed up to the edge of the tower. Sixty feet doesn't look very high from the ground, but backing up to jump off while looking down seems like a long way to the ground.

"How in the heck do I get started", I said as I looked down. "Just jump out and let some rope out as you do", said Lt. Hill. Well I found that easier said than done, so as I awkwardly started out, I found my feet remaining on the edge of the tower while the rest of me went totally upside down, hanging on that rope. I finally managed to get my footing and pull myself up to about a 90 degree angle, and jumped out, released some rope finally realizing how it worked. Whew!

Next, it was back up on the other side of the tower where there was no boarding. I hooked up the ropes to my D-Ring, stepped back on a fixed chopper skid and just jumped

Dick Rappelling and Slack Jumping off a sixty foot high tower. This training was many times rigged up to keep us well honed, and of course occupied during our stand-downs

with the first pull being after a 20 foot drop due to the slack left in the rope; thus slack jumping. The rest of the way down you just try to gauge your drop distances until you get to the ground. Obviously when under fire you go as fast as possible and make sure you pull up before hitting the ground. When jumping in a clear zone it's safer to drop in several pull-ups which control your speed of descent to the ground.

After this training, we were given the rest of the day off and enjoyed the hot food of the base camp, and in this case we cooked some great steaks and ribs. Oh and of course we would drink some beer. Did I say some beer, well I guess it was more like a lot of beer, so much so that later that night I found my cot in my tent and passed out.

SSG. Johnson cooking steaks for the guys on stand-down. Barbeques were great fellowship times for any Bands of Brothers, and we always looked forward to them. A great break from C-rations.

Sometime about 0200 hours, the silence in the basecamp, other than the continual noise of the generators that one gets used to, was broken by rockets coming in on top of us. The engineers had dug a ditch all along the front of the company area where we could seek shelter in the event of incoming.

"Dick…Mac…McBain" was being yelled at me by some of the guys as these rockets were coming in around us. I began to wake from a drunken stupor and a rocket hit very near me. "Shhhhhhhhboom", was the deafening noise and the bright white flash in the dark near my tent really woke me up. "Dick…common…common…get in the trench", was the call from the guys, and after the rocket hit close, I was needing no further prodding. I jumped up, ran as fast as I could and dove in the trench. After they stopped coming in, we began to laugh at how ridiculous I was to be so wasted

Dick in tent resting during Stand-down, the day before the rocket attack which practically blew him out of his cot and shaming him for being so drunk. Cots seemed comfortable after sleeping on the ground

that I couldn't even hear the rockets at first. "Hey, this ain't supposed to happen on our stand-down", someone said, and was answered by several other guys, "Don't mean nothin', and der it is breeze"!

The accuracy of incoming and the enemy knowing we were in for a couple of days used to amaze me until several Vietnamese "civilians" who worked in the base camp were apprehended walking off distances to our tents and sizing up our being there for a stand-down.

The fact that the Army hired Gooks from the area to work in the base camps always bothered me. It seemed that we were just asking for trouble letting this go on, and we were told they did it to handle the jobs the troops didn't want to do. My next question was, "Then why are we burning crap?"

A couple of months before this incident, we heard while we were out in the boonies, that they had caught some gook "employees" walking, or should I say pacing off the footsteps to where they parked the choppers. I never could understand why they didn't learn from these incidents. We shortly went back to the tents and back to sleep.

Larry Dent, unknown brother, Dick McBain & Ed Matajesyk talking in a tent during stand-down. Instead of always having to be alert together, these times allowed us to let our hair down so to speak, and really get to know each other

The next morning a few of us went to the little "gook" shops inside the base camp. They had a number of these little stores, one of which was some sort of tailor shop. It was commonly frequented by our troops to have our new jungle uniform shirts embroidered with our name, U.S. Army, and CIB's if we had them. It seemed to me almost everyone did this as the cheap name patch and U.S. Army patch that were on the fatigues looked real cheap.

Gook shops in Camp Eagle provided several services such as tailoring, stores with wide varieties of items soldiers want like lighters, waterproof wallets, and knives. There was also a legitimate massage parlor

Of course our Boonie hats were also an item most liked to get embroidered. Everyone had their own wording done or CIB's put on them. Some had their states name put on them, and some had our unit "Strike Force" put on them, but it was rare to see a Boonie hat without something on it. Many of the guys had grenade pins attached all around the hat band.

Some of the shops had various and sundry items that were of interest to soldiers. One of the main small items that were very popular were the cigarette lighters. A large number of the soldiers smoked in those days, and lighters were just a standard need.

They had a number of lighters, but the most popular for us

were the Zippo's with the Screaming Eagle emblem on the side. They also had some with engraving on the other side, which said, "When I die I'll go to Heaven, 'cause I've spent my time in Hell". Then of course the one's with the para-phrased scripture, "Yea thought I walk thru the valley of the shadow of death, I will fear no evil, For I am the Airborne Infantry, and I'm the baddest M F'er in the Valley" (only spelled out) There were also shops with camera's, watches, film, and water proof wallets with the Screaming Eagle patch, Guitars, and many other items.

Bill Nelson and some of the others, "Muff", Richard Hayman, and Ray Nyman were friends and brothers and all of us enjoyed the time together at stand-downs

Out in the boonies we had no time for racism. There could be arguments that would start from time to time, but we were too busy watching out for each other to let something like racism get in the way. In the rear areas, it was different. There seemed to be a lot of racism going on, at least in the sense of the different races hanging out with each other, and intermingling periodically when off duty. As a matter of fact the "Pound" had been born, and guys that were racist didn't like the white guys to participate in the pound at all.

The pound was in place of a handshake, where the two people would put out their right fist, then begin a ritual of first pounding down on one fist, then the other pounding down on the other's fist. The various assortments of fists tapping together, bouncing up each other's forearm and then clicking the fingers as you got to the top. When I first got to the Nam, the pound was a short mixture of some of that stuff. By the time I was leaving, the pound could go on for minutes with ridiculous movements of arms and body.

One time when we were just in for stand-down, we headed to the mess hall to get our first warm meal in over a month. Our black brothers sat with us as we were all together. Some of the rear guys came up to the table, and said to our black guys, "Common brother, give me the pound". One of our guys looked up and said, "My brother, this is the first hot food I have had in a month. I will be glad to shake your hand, but I'm not about to let my food get cold while we go through all of those pound motions you guys do back here". "You ain't no brother of mine", came the response. "Fine, have it your way", our guy said and continued eating.

In the boonies we all played around with the pound, and sometimes tried to get as ridiculous as we could, to be funny. However it was all in fun and we meant no disrespect in clowning around with it, and our black brothers knew that.

CHAPTER SEVEN

KIT CARSON SCOUT – TONG LON DIEP

One operation my platoon had been chosen to be the lead element to move out and clear the way for the rest of the company. Lt. Richardson, our new platoon leader decided that he was going to have Diep (Ton Lon Diep), our Kit Carson Scout walk point. Now in theory it was a perfectly normal expectation.

Tong Lon Diep was a captured VC (Viet Cong) enemy soldier who became a scout for our company. He was a worthless scout, but we all liked him so he just stayed with us

A Kit Carson Scout was a former NVA or VC (enemy) soldier who had "Chieu Hoi'd" (surrendered) to us, and had been given the choice of going to Kit Carson Scout School and becoming a scout for us, or being a POW behind bars. Diep was smart enough to choose the later, and became a scout…"choke…choke"…for us. The problem was we could never get Diep to do anything he perceived as being dangerous, and walking point was dangerous. Some units, especially the Marines made them do what they wanted or might shoot them if they didn't, but we all had grown fond of Diep and just sort of let him get by.

Earlier at one of our resupply's, Diep had the surprise of his life. I had been able to get to know him for a few months or so, and always felt bad for him when they would get mail out to us knowing he would never get any because his family was in North, Vietnam, land of our enemies. I wrote my Mom and asked her to send a second package of goodies boxed separately, and addressed to Ton Long Diep at our unit.

We were eating dinner one evening after they had brought us a resupply in the afternoon. Someone brought around the mail and was calling out names. "Ton Long Diep", yelled the mail guy. Diep looked up real fast and couldn't believe he had heard his name for mail. The guy handed him a box about 2 feet square with his name on it. Everybody gathered around to watch him, and he was told by the mail guy it was from the McBain's in Dayton, Ohio. He knew that name was mine and he looked at me with tears in his eyes. "Go ahead, open it", came the cry from a couple of the guys. He did and found just what I had in mine; cookies, some candy, and other goodies my Mom made to send me. . It was very heartwarming to watch him, and he later thanked me heartily.

"Scout Diep, front and center", the Lt. commanded. Diep came running like a good obedient soldier until he was told to "take the point", by the Lieutenant. He turned half white as he knew it was likely we would run into the enemy, and point-men often get shot if we do. Diep was smart enough not to argue, but had no intention of walking point. "Ah, OK Sir" he mumbled and without waiting for his "slack-man" (second in line who covered the point-man) he quickly headed out.

Lt. Morehead thought it was a good thing that he moved out so quickly, but he and all who knew Diep were sure something was up. The rest of the lead element began to move out in this triple-canopy jungle and were out about a hundred meters or so before the call came in that they had not met up with the point man. What had happened was that Diep moved out quickly until he was out of sight in the jungle, then circled back to the rear of our lead platoon.

The radios were humming…"Where the hell is Diep", the Lieutenant called up to us in front. "We have zero contact

Company RTO & Capt. Faulkenberry calling ahead to see what the holdup was. Diep was missing, or should I say hiding

with point, over", was my response as I had a radio. Then all hell broke loose! "Trover Five this is Trover one, what in hell is going on up there", came the angry response from the CO, Capt. Faulkenberry. "We've lost contact with our point man and trying to find him, over", said the LT. "Five, you find that point man and get this unit moving, out", the CO commanded. "Roger", was the subdued response from LT.

Someone from the platoon saw Diep sitting toward the rear of the line and grabbed him by his belt dragging him up front to Lt. Morehead's position. "What do you think you're doing", Lt. yelled at Diep. "No Bic", came the quick response from Diep, meaning he did not speak English and could not understand. This was a favorite expression of any Vietnamese if they found themselves in a bad position.

Diep did not speak very good English, but he always seemed to understand what he was told unless he didn't want to understand. Rather than fight with language problems, Lt called ahead and just told the unit to move out with the next man walking point. I never saw anyone tell Diep to walk point again, probably because it was felt he would do a lousy job of it anyway, and the point man was very important.

We set up later that day in a beautiful area on a hundred foot hill overlooking a crystal clear river. Some of the best water I have ever tasted in my life was in those mountain spring fed rivers in northern South Vietnam. There was a deep pool in the river right by us, and the river ran fast on the rocks as it came down from the mountain.

The next day I came down to the river with a couple of buddies to fill our canteens, and saw Diep squatting near the water working on something. "Hey Diep", I shouted over the noise of the river, which startled him and he turned quickly with his M-16 toward me. I brought my rifle up fast as for a brief moment I was just reacting. When he saw it was me, he quickly dropped the front of his rifle and got a big smile on his face. "What are you up to", I said as I was curious about what he was doing.

He showed me a fishhook he had made from the large black safety pin that came pinned to every bandoleer of M-16 ammo. He had molded it and cut a barb on the hook end, and it look just like a fish hook you would buy in a store. He has fashioned a line from something, and put some kind of bait on it and threw it in the deep pool. He was nodding his head up and down saying, "Numba One…Numba One", which I interpreted to mean he was going to catch us some fish to eat.

A few minutes later one of the guys came down the trail to us and said, "We're getting ready to move out". When he saw Diep fishing with his little drop line, he went up to him and said, "Diep, that's not the way you fish in this unit"! He then pulled a grenade, pulled the pin and threw it in the deep pool. We all jumped back and BOOM, water splashed ten feet into the air, and a few fish came floating to the surface. "That's the way we fish around here", he said. Unfortunately it was a waste as we headed up the trail to get ready to move out.

Later that year in the dry season we were humping through the jungle, up and down the large "Hills" and were running out of water. We were sent off in different directions to try and find a "Blue Line" (river) that had not dried up. Our lips were parched and white, and every time we found a river, it would be a dried up riverbed. It became so bad that

I remember seeing Diep cut a large leaf off a tree, then urinating into it and drinking it. "I'm not that thirsty yet", I said to some of the guys with me. "Almost, but not quite". We managed to climb to the top of a mountain, and found a small clear spot with grass to sit down. We were so thoroughly dehydrated that we ended up lying in the grass and trying to make jokes.

"Man, just think, I started, "back in the world people are just walking down the hall to the water fountain and getting all they want of clear, cool water". "McBain, shut-up" came a response from several of my buddies. Then someone else would start, "Wouldn't you like to dive into a clear pool of water right about now". "Oh man, shut-up, what's wrong with you guys", some would moan.

The Lt. finally caught up with us on the top of the hill, and realized something needed to be done. He called the CO to let him know of our dyer situation without water in 98 degrees. "I didn't know you men were that low on water", was his response. "I will call in for an emergency kick-out" he said.

We were glad he was doing that but a little ticked off he was not sitting in our position. He had plenty of water because he was not out climbing huge hills in jungle trying to find water, and ours had run out because of his orders.

The next happening was almost inexcusable. "Strike Force Five, Strike Force Five, this is Remy Two, over", came the call from the chopper bringing out water. "Remy two, Strike Force Five, we will pop yellow smoke at our location, over", answered the Lt. Yellow smoke was popped, the chopper acknowledged it, and he said, "We are kicking out some ice to hold you until they can get out here soon with a water blivit, over".

A water blivit was a very hard, maybe one or two inch thick rubber container about two feet high and two or three feet wide. It could be kicked out of a chopper for emergency water resupply from probably 50 feet or so and remain intact. It probably held 25 gallons of water. "Roger", said the Lt. "OK, look up and watch where it lands as we don't want to hit you with the ice", said the pilot.

Yellow smoke grenade was popped to let the chopper pilot know it was ok to come in, or over us in this case. Different colors of smoke could be used except red. That meant hot LZ and under fire

The chopper began to hover near us, but for some reason, just as they were kicking out the ice, the chopper moved abruptly away from us and over the chasm between our hill and another. We watched as the ice fell hundreds of feet down to the bottom of the mountain. One of the guys picked up his rifle and looked like he was going to shoot at the chopper, but came to his senses in time. We were furious, and the pilot didn't know what to say. I'm sure he could see our ranting as he pulled over us, and said how sorry he was and flew away.

We sat for five or ten minutes just cussing up a storm and trying to decide if we should go after the ice. We decided that it would be melted by the time we got to it, and did not go but had great news a few minutes later. "Strike Force Five this is Taffey Niner, over" came a call on the radio. "Taffey Niner this is Five, over, replied the LT. We've got a water blivit for you guys and need smoke popped at your location", said the pilot. We popped smoke, made sure he knew just where to kick out the blivit, and all went well. All the water we needed and then some, Thank God.

After refreshing ourselves for a while, we moved back down the hillside and continued our patrol. We came to some abandoned bunkers and immediately went into a defensive perimeter around them. LT called up Diep to get his former enemy opinion on what we were dealing with here. "Diep, are these NVA or VC?" the LT asked. Diep rose up from a prone position next to the Lieutenant and looked very slowly and carefully at the area. Then he answered, "Maybe VC....maybe NVA". LT said, "Somebody hit this idiot", as he was frustrated that Diep never seem to know anything or do anything of any value to us, but we kept him anyway.

Later that week one of the point guys hit a trip wire across the trail and blew a booby-trap. He wasn't killed but was wounded and medevac'd. When it happened, we were told to get down and take a break.

Tom Brennan taking a break while medics tended to the wounded man who hit the booby-trap. He smiled for my picture, but none of us were happy about our injured brother

Usually I would hit my quick-release buckles on my rucksack to drop it quickly to the ground, and then sit on my helmet leaning up against my ruck. That time I was tired enough to just plop down on the ground with the ruck still on, but as I did so I felt the weight of the rucksack pulling me backward.

I managed to grab onto something and looked over my shoulder. I had plopped down at the very edge of a hidden pungi-pit on the side of the trail, and the weight of my rucksack was over the edge of the pit drawing me in. I managed to pull myself away and got up to take a look. It was a small pungi-pit only about three feet deep, with five or six pungi-stakes sticking up. This small a pit was not intended to kill but to injure and poison.

Pungi-pits were many different sizes dug by the enemy to either kill GI's or wound them badly enough to get them out of the field. The big ones could be many feet deep with ten or twenty pungi-stakes in them which would cause soldiers to fall into and be impaled by the pungi-stakes. The pungi-stakes were usually coated on their spears with human excrement to create infection to survivors. This pit was designed to have a troop step in thus ramming the stake through the boot necessitating a medevac.

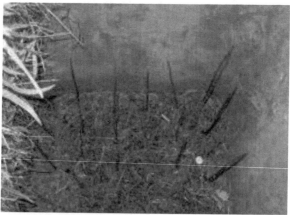

Small Pungi-pit containing stakes covered with excrement to cause infection to the unlucky victim stepping in it. I almost sat in one like this one

In "Hot" AO's we usually tried to cut our way through the jungle to avoid using existing trails, if any. This was much more difficult and slower, but we avoided boob-traps and other killing devices. The enemy used many types of these devices to take a toll on American troops who would utilize these existing trails. Grenades tied to a tree or bamboo with a hidden trip wire, pungi-stakes mounted on a board attached to a tree limb and pulled back then connected to a trip wire that would swing swiftly impaling the soldier, and little anti-personnel mines were some of their favorites.

One of the things Diep did know was the enemy's use of booby-traps and other surprises. He probably saved my butt, and some of the other guys more than once in stopping us just before triggering one. He could spot them much more easily than I could, and Diep turned out to be a friend we could depend on in those situations. What always griped us more was finding that many of these booby traps were made from our equipment, meaning some GI's were careless about discarding their stuff in a proper way.

I always felt sorry for Diep because he had a wife and children in the North, and knew he would be very lucky if he ever saw them again. I hope he did!

CHAPTER EIGHT

2nd FIVE O'Deuce – STRIKE FORCE
THE READY REACTION FORCE

It seemed we had more names than we needed, and another was the "Ready Reaction Force", which meant if elements of our battalion needed help in a combat situation, we would be sent to get them out; sometime being extracted from one area and then CA'd to another.

One such time we were in the rear area for a stand-down and Top Manning came to us and said, "Second Platoon is being sent on a "Life-Saver" mission to secure a unit of engineers who are clearing a new fire support base, and have taken some enemy small arms fire. Take your ruck sacks and full resupply as I don't know how long you'll be there", he continued. "A Chinook (CH-47 double bladed helicopter) will be taking you out to secure the area around them".

We packed our gear and headed up to the chopper pad. The Chinook came in and we climbed aboard for a short trip out to the engineers. "I don't like these Chinooks", I said to Shorty, "I like quick exits from the Slicks (Huey Helicopters) that we can just jump out of". Little did I know that this was going to be a new experience none of us were prepared for, nor had done previously.

The chopper arrived at the location and we found there had not been much work done by the engineers in clearing an LZ. They had popped green smoke to say it was OK to come in, but into where? I soon found out!

As the Chinook hovered, the tailgate began to lower, and one of the crew threw a large rope ladder out of the rear. "What the hell is this", I asked rather angrily. "You guys are going to have to go down the ladder because we can't land", was the response from the crew member. I looked over the edge of the tailgate and said, "Oh hell no"! "Yea, sorry but get going", was the unsympathetic response.

We were hovering about 50 feet above the ground, and the rope ladder was just swinging with the wind of the chopper's blades. I put my ruck sack on and slung my rifle, and grabbed hold of the rope ladder. Tom Brennan, our squad leader said, "I'll go first", and started his descent. After he was about half of the way down I started out on the ladder when Jaco said, "I'm not going down that thing", as strongly as he could, but I quickly snapped back, "If I'm going – you're going; get your stuff on. When we get to the bottom we'll do our best to hold the ladder making it easier for you guys to get down", I said.

This would have been a perfect situation for slack-jumping, but we weren't prepared with the needed equipment because the chopper pilot thought he would be able to land at the site.

As I began down the ladder, the weight of my ruck sack caused my feet to be practically at a 45 degree angle or worse, above me at times. I hung on for dear life as I slowly but methodically descended mostly using my hands and arm strength. I looked down and saw that Tom had made it and was doing what he could to hold the bottom of the rope ladder. After what seemed like forever, I managed to get my feet on the ground. It was even more difficult as the chopper was lifting and falling with the wind, and sometimes we would be lifted right off the ground holding onto that ladder, but soon we had everyone on the ground.

Much to our surprise the crew of the Chinook opened the tailgate, threw out a rope ladder, and told us to get going down on the ladder because they couldn't land

The good news was that we hadn't been shot at coming down the ladder by the two gooks that were harassing the engineers earlier. We spread out a little bit and waited to see if any firing was done. There was none and we figured they had di di mau'd when our chopper got above them. They were most likely a couple of trail-watchers who never put up a fight with larger numbers

Trail-watchers usually travelled in two's and they were like scouts way out from their unit whose job was to search for enemy units and report back afterward.

"Dick take Jaco and Tony with you and go secure the far

side of the hill out in front of those engineers over there", Tom said while pointing.

Securing the area anytime we were going to be somewhere for a period of time was always first on the agenda. This was done by setting up fire lane positions in a perimeter around who we were securing

Ten minutes later we had made sure that the area was secured, and the engineers continued on with their work. They already had a bulldozer and a terrain vehicle there, which another Chinook had lowered down to them through the trees before they received enemy fire, but once we got there we had no more trouble.

Although it's not spoken of much, there are always the necessities of life that needs to be taken care of in the boonies, whether in a clear AO or hot. Too often were the times when you had to go, knowing the enemy was around. I hated that because no one wanted to get killed, especially while taking a dump. Troopers could get killed by their own guys if they didn't let those on guard know where they were going and that they would be out doing their thing. We usually took our entrenching tool with us, dug what we called a cat hole, and then covered it up and quickly headed back into the perimeter.

I always wondered how many times in a year Charlie was out there watching just wanting to blow me away while I was vulnerable. In real hot battle situations we might just dig a latrine within the perimeter for safety's sake, but I don't remember that being allowed much.

When we would get low on water, we would send out a squad to make a water run for the whole platoon. We'd leave our rucksacks and most of the other stuff, and carry our rifles, two bandoleers of ammo, and a bunch of canteens tied together. The canteens were plastic and didn't clang with noise. When we'd arrive at the stream, we'd set up a small perimeter and cover the two or so guys who would fill the canteens, and if we were really hot we take turns bathing with soap in the stream after the water was collected.

Usually, the streams and rivers where we mostly operated in the northern hills of South Vietnam had clear, great tasting water in them. We had pills we were supposed to use to kill the germs, but I don't remember using them. Now the units in the lowlands had to use them as the water there was many times stagnant or contaminated with farm runoff. Up north where we were the water was generally crystal clean, and some of the best water I had ever tasted.

Sometime later we were extracted and landed on another FSB. From there we were trucked north of Hue, the Provincial Capital, and would run some reconnaissance-in-force operations near Quang Tri. The trucks let us off somewhere in that area and it was a mixture of different terrain. Some areas were more open and not covered with jungle, which made it easier to move in. We went out in both squad and platoon size missions with the intent to make contact with the enemy and kill them or to find any

Caches of weapons they may have hid. What was funny was that most of us hoped we didn't make contact so we wouldn't get killed either.

This is the first time I had been in the Quang Tri area and we ran into one of our mechanized units along the road. It seemed strange seeing our tanks along a jungle road, and we stopped for a short time while our officers conversed with some of the mechanized officers. We shared a cigarette or two with the tank guys then got on our way.

There had evidently been some intelligence that weapons caches were thought to have been buried or hidden in the area, sometimes in villages, and our mission was to see if we could find any. We had some small finds of which were probably planted a little over a year ago for the Tet offensive. We were very near Hue and of course that was the location of an intense battle during Tet with the 101st and the Marines. In preparing for these coordinated attacks, the gooks would bury or hide small caches in and around the areas they were targeting to have the materials handy. With these smaller finds, the weapons, if any, were sent to the rear and the rest of the ordinance we gathered and blew up in place.

It was in these types of operations that we got a chance to better know some of the other guys in our unit, especially operating in platoon strength. You always knew everybody in your platoon, but mostly only got close to the guys in your squad. The reason was you were always alongside your squad guys for patrols, guard duty, and down time, while the other guys in the platoon were of course hanging with their squad guys. In this kind of operation it seemed the squads worked more closely together, and therefore you had the chance to find out more about the others.

Bob Lawson, Steve Clement, Doc Shenk, Richard Hayman, and "Buck" Watson posing with an enemy weapons cache' we discovered in the jungle. Numerous RPG's (Rocket Propelled Grenades), mortar rounds, and other weapons including a machine gun were found

  Some of the men were more serious than others, and I was one of a number of us that liked to joke around to take the "edge off". Bill Nelson, a machine-gunner in second platoon and I hit it off when I first got to the company. He had been there a few months before me, and treated me like an "equal" instead of a "Cherry" that so many others loved to chide me about. Being a new guy can be intimidating in an already stressful situation, but Bill and Steve Clement treated me like one of them and both liked to joke around which really helped break the tension. From that time on, when we got together we would joke about some of the

Bill Nelson – machine gunner and good friend. Bill was one of the guys who tried to make my "Cherryhood" easier by treating me like everyone else. Cherry's, or new guys, usually got quite a bit of initiation until baptized in a firefight

guys like Nelson Reyes, who always slept with his eyes wide open, or Sergeant Major Sabalauski who would always bust our chops about haircuts the minute we arrived in the rear.

Sometimes we would just sit around and talk about how weird it seemed to be here carrying guns and rocket launchers on our person, while just several months ago we were home, and I was sitting in some class at college with not a care in the world but passing the courses and who to ask out for a date next week. The change was obviously stark and sometimes hard to comprehend.

Basic training had broken us of our civilian ways, and now the real life and death situation daily seemed hard to believe. All of us were determined to do our duty while in country, but our main longing and goal was to get home alive. The guys who were nearing the end of their tour were determined to be what we called "Short" when they got to thirty days left in the Nam. We called them short-timers and they were given a Short-Timers Calendar where they marked off the days to going home. If you were short, you were envied and given an extra layer of respect.

One of the worse things that could happen to morale was when a Short-timer was killed. We of course grieved for him and how close he was to making it, but it also told us we would not be safe until the plane lifted off from Vietnam soil to make the trip home. I saw far too many Short-timers either get killed or wounded badly to have much hope of "making it" until my last day. It was something we did not dwell on, but was always on our minds.

CHAPTER NINE

INCOMING

It was a beautiful day in early March of 1970 in the mountainous region of Northern I Corps. We were on a summit slightly above the lower cloud line on Fire Support Base Veghel. Our temporary job was to secure the artillery company that was in support of the operations of our battalion in the area. We were surrounded by mountains covered with triple canopy jungle, and were grateful for this brief reprieve of living in the jungle, where we could now get some hot food while being on the firebase. That feeling of gratitude for firebase hot food was soon to be discarded with an enemy setting up an unwelcome surprise not far from us.

Typical FSB (Fire Support Base) with open hill top for artillery pieces, also causing a wide open target for Charlie to drop mortar rounds on whenever the spirit moved him

The morning was silent and peaceful as we went about our duties of checking the claymores, trip flares, cleaning our weapons, and joking around. "Hey Caje, I'll bet Jody is back on the block messing with your girl", someone said. "Ya man, when I git back on the block, ol' Jody be plenty sorry, I garuntee", Cajun replied back. We laughed at his accent, and were glad for a little break from humping eighty to hundred pound plus ruck sacks up and down these hills, and cutting our way through bamboo, razor sharp elephant grass and "wait-a-minute" vines.

"Caje" Farrell Faul posing with a "Thumper" (M-79 Grenade Launcher) that looked like a short barrel over-extended single shot shotgun, that broke open like one and you loaded the grenade round and fired

"What the hell is that", I said as I looked over next to an ammo box and saw this large, ugly, purple something that was about 8" long, with a body about ½ inch wide and was purple, with many thick orange legs. "Oh that's a centipede", came a response, "and be careful 'cause they're poisonous", another said.

I had never seen anything like it and I threw something at it. That monster insect moved toward me like a rocket, I mean unbelievably fast. I managed to step on its rear part with my boot, and its front end reared up and began

Centipede with fangs could move very quickly and strike like a snake. They were poisonous and something no one wanted to mess with. Blondie was bitten between the eyes in the jungle by one and had to be medevac'd, but turned out ok

striking my boot with its fangs, just like a snake striking. Someone grabbed a machete and cut it in two. I could not believe my eyes, and little did I know I would see many things like it in the jungle. One of these bit "Blondie" between the eyes later on in the year, and his forehead swelled out approximately two inches over his eyes. He was medevac'd but was OK.

Each unit prided itself on doing certain things that required toughness and physical determination, and we were no different. I knew I was in for it when I first arrived

Dick with rucksack which was approximately 125 pounds carrying three gallons of water, case of c-rations, PRC 25 radio, LAW rocket launchers on back, plus ammo

at the 101st basecamp in Vietnam and saw the billboard that stated "They've got us surrounded the poor bastards". My chagrin only increased when I noticed on the door of each "Hooch" in the camp that there was a painted silhouette of a soldier bent over forward with this huge ruck sack on his back. I soon found out those pictures were no joke.

Hey Steve, "what are we drinking" I said as I could see he was heating up some hot chocolate. Before he could answer we were confronted with an all too familiar sound coming from the jungle. Thump…thump…thump broke the stillness as in the near distance the distinct noise of enemy mortar tubes was heard by those of us paying attention.

"INCOMING...INCOMING ", I and several others yelled at the top of our lungs as men began to scramble everywhere to try and find a hole. KAVOOM - KAVOOM was the shattering noise as mortar shells hit all around us. I will never understand why some men would stand up while trying to spot where the tubes were firing from, but some always did. Many of us would yell at them to get down, trying to remind them of the imminent danger. Some would finally wake-up, but many times those that didn't would be hit. This day was no exception, and as the explosions continued I heard the screams of those hit yelling that sound you just did not want to hear, "Medic, Medic".

The mortar attack lasted all of five minutes before breaking off, as the gooks knew we would be zeroing in on their positions, and return fire with our 105's and 155 howitzers. Sometimes we were fast enough to get them, but not today. They decided to di di mau out of the area quickly as they knew what it was like when the Americans would bring "the world" down on top of them. Never the less, our artillery company powdered the area in the direction we knew they were firing from just to remind them that the 101st Airborne Division never took a fight sitting down.

While our guns were firing back, a number of us got out of our holes to get to the wounded and stop their bleeding. No one was killed that day, but a few were wounded, and unfortunately, it had to be considered all in a day's work. "Just another day in the Nam...don't mean nothin", someone said, and we all reluctantly knew he was right.

Other than the hot food, most of us preferred our jungle living where we weren't just wide open targets for the enemy to hit and run. We knew some squad was going to have to go out and recon to see if we hit the enemy with the artillery, and that quickly happened.

Platoon Sergeant Johnson came over and quickly assembled our squad. "Second Squad, take an extra bandoleer with you and leave all the other junk here", he said, "and keep your heads down". We headed out toward the direction of the firing, and after half a click (500 meters) we had found the evidence of our artillery shells explosions, but found no blood trails to indicate that any of the enemy had been hit.

Hitting the enemy without any idea of where they were firing from, except the direction, was a one in a million shot. We all realized that but we had to check out the area to make sure there wasn't something larger out there. We searched all around looking for blood trails but found none. We decided with no luck to head back to the fire base.

As we started back, there was a mixed feeling of being glad we didn't run into a firefight, but also anger that we didn't have the opportunity to kill those who tried to kill us. As we approached the firebase from the thick jungle, we yelled our password several times, "Strike force… Strike force…..Strike force" to alert the trail guards not to fire on us as we exited the heavy cover to the open firebase area. Many times the guys guarding the trail didn't have a radio so we always made sure they knew when we left, and approximately when we would be returning. We told them if they were relieved before we got back to tell the new guards we were out there and coming back

Patrol searching along a dried up "Blue Line" (River) trying to find some sign of the enemy. Travelling in the open areas provided by rivers was risky but much quicker, so they were often taken

All of that "telling" seemed to be much ado about nothing, but out in the boonies many guys get itchy trigger fingers when they hear noises approaching, and if they haven't been told, it might mean another friendly fire incident.

Back on the firebase we muddled around trying to keep our minds off of the morning's attack. As my time in Vietnam increased, it seemed that I had found a way of anesthetizing my feelings to help me deal with the loss of friends and be able to do my job.

That night we were told that we would have one "Mad-Minute", which was a time when everyone of the securing infantry company would open up around the hill with machineguns, rifles, pop-up flares, all at once exhibiting extensive firepower in the event that the enemy was creeping up or even just watching our hill from the jungle. It was quite a display, and we enjoyed doing it as it seemed to give us a chance to let off some steam.

Now we jungle fighters were often called "Booney-Rats" by others from the rear areas. It was a name we liked, and were proud to be called. I had heard that the name came from the huge rats that were in the jungle, but little did I know how huge until my first Mad-Minute on my first Firebase.

When I had first come out to the company in November of 1969, the company was on FSB Rifle. That day I was warned of the boney-rats that came up on the FSB at night to get into the trash sumps for food. I though the guys were just pulling this "Cherry's" leg, but man did I find out different that night.

As the mad- minute began, and the pop-up flares were fired, the rats would run all around us trying to get out of the light. These rats were approximately two feet long and the size of a small dog or a huge cat. I was really freaked out when I first saw them, and when we went to sleep on the ground on these firebases, they would run right over you in the dark. Oddly enough it was just another thing in the Nam that you would have to get used to.

During the "Mad-Minute" almost everyone would fire their weapons, and the "Quad-fifties" (four fifty caliber machine guns mounted on a turret would open up; the noise was almost deafening. Then the artillery guys on the top of the hill would shout down to us, "Get your heads down" as they lowered their howitzers to ground level. "Fire in the hole", was yelled three times to give us final warning, then they would fire right over our heads using what was called "Beehive" rounds containing 8,000 "Fleshettes", which were like a huge shotgun shells.

Our artillery had "Beehive" rounds that contained four to eight thousand "Fleshettes" which were short, steel arrows. These were fired like shotgun shells in a frontal attack, and could pin the enemy to a tree

The "Fleshettes" that came out of the artillery guns were miniature steel arrows, lots of them in each round fired, and they would literally pin any enemy "sappers" to the trees behind them. These arrows had the arrow head, shaft, and steel feathers just like actual hunting arrows. When the Mad-minute was over, everything became dark again and we all returned to our positions for sleeping or guard duty. During my first couple of Mad-Minutes the adrenaline from all the explosions and firing would keep me up for a while, but after that it was just "old hat".

After a few days we were told we were moving out, and we all packed our C's, ammo, and such for our next operation in the boonies. We gathered at the chopper pad and the CO gave us a briefing of where we were going. I pulled a little laughing machine out of my rucksack that my Dad had sent in a package from home, and turned it on. It was hilarious laughter coming from the machine and soon had everyone else laughing except the CO. When I saw he was not amused, I quickly turned it off and put it away, and he never said anything to me about it. However, I do believe it really helped some of us who were worried about the upcoming operation to relieve some tension, and laughter almost always has that affect.

We all lined up in sortie order around the chopper pad, and we saw the familiar long line of choppers that were bringing in the next company to secure the firebase, while taking us out to our AO. Each chopper would come in with the troops jumping off, and then we would jump on with the choppers lifting off taking us to our next mission. Bringing in the troops was called an extraction, and those being taken to an AO was called a CA (Combat Assault).

Standard Operating Procedure for a combat assault was that firebase artillery would blow up the area on and around the LZ we were going in to about five to ten minutes before we arrived. Cobra gunships would accompany our choppers, and as we started going in they would fire up the area with rockets and min-guns. The purpose was of course to kill any enemy waiting in ambush, but also to set off any booby-traps positioned by the enemy.

The first guys on the first few birds would usually jump off a few feet off the ground and run spreading out and firing up the area in front of them. This was done not only to get the gooks heads down if there were any around, but to draw fire from them if they were there so the Cobras could be called in to level the area the enemy was in.

After the initial troop landing and all was secure, the others came into the LZ where everyone was scurrying around as usual to quickly unload people and materials clearing the

Combat Assault where choppers brought troops in to a LZ for combat operations in an AO, and quickly dropped them off, many times not even touching the ground

way for each chopper that was coming in. Once everybody was on the ground, the CO called the platoon leaders to his location and selected a platoon to be in the lead. He would then give them map coordinates to our next objective, and the lead squad of the selected platoon would move out.

CHAPTER TEN

DRUGS IN VIETNAM

The extreme pressures in a war zone can cause men and women to do things they might otherwise not even consider. Besides the pressures of trying to stay alive in combat, there is a great deal of boredom, especially in the rear areas where most are on shifts. They find little to do when off duty so they look for ways to pass the time.

In Vietnam, drugs were easy to find and in many cases overlooked by the MP's as no a big deal. Not to say there were none, but I never remember hearing about one single drug bust in our unit the whole year I was in the Nam.

In the jungle I really wanted to keep my head together for the obvious need of instant readiness, and most of us felt that way. There were times that someone would present a joint or two, and we would decide if we were someplace we didn't really have to worry about an attack. Of course those of us who did the considering were former pot smokers back home or since coming to Vietnam, while others who had not used or even tried marijuana thought that we were nuts.

In Vietnam there were basically three types of soldiers when it came to getting high; the drinkers, the "heads", and those who did both. The drinkers stuck to the use of alcohol when on stand-downs, or in the rear while on duty there. The "Heads" were the pot or opium smokers, who also did other drugs when available like Obenzedrine. Those who did both comprised of, in my estimation, around thirty to forty percent of personnel, at least on occasion.

In the jungle we very rarely saw any alcohol and when we did, it was warm beer brought out on resupply at the request of the CO for one reason or another. On those occasions you were fortunate to get one or possibly two cans of beer, but it was usually so warms that I personally didn't care for it.

Pot was usually in pre-rolled joints and easy to find, or even brought to us by the kids when we would get close to their villages. You could buy a small package of ten joints rolled up neatly and sealed in a clear plastic pouch for ten dollars. The quality was very good as far as getting you high, and kids selling joints were just trying to make a few extra bucks.

One day we had been out in the boonies for a month or so, and had moved into what was considered a quiet AO, meaning there was little to no enemy activity expected in the area. It was a clear, beautiful day and we had been set up in this particular position for a few days. The guys on duty were all at their watch positions, and of course all of the claymore mines, trip flares, and other weapons had all been in place since we set up there a few days prior.

Four or five of us were sitting around in a small clearing shooting the bull and enjoying the weather. As we were discussing our thoughts about when we would be moving out, and where we might be going based on the scuttlebutt that was heard here and there, someone produced a couple of joints. There seemed to be quick agreement to light them up and pass them around as we hadn't had any sign of the enemy, or contact in a week or so. Out came the zippo lighter and we were off and running. I walked across the clearing to where the joints were being passed, leaving my M-16 resting up against a blown down tree, something I rarely did. It was usually hard to catch me without my rifle in my hand, or being laid at my side.

After a short time we five were loaded, and I mean stoned. We were talking about all kinds of things and of course got the marijuana giggles, where you laugh hard until you hurt. Some began opening up c-ration cans with the big chocolate and coconut bar in them to satisfy the munchies we were getting. Everyone was very relaxed and having an enjoyable time.

I was sitting on the ground in the quiet listening to the birds when out of nowhere, BOOM, a huge blast broke the silence and shook the air and leaves around us. No matter how loaded you were, your training automatically takes over, and the first thought I had was we were under attack, and I reached for my weapon. It wasn't where I always laid it, and I was in the prone position scurrying around on the ground trying to find my weapon.

It turned out that it had fallen with the blast behind the tree that I had laid it against and I couldn't see it. I began to panic believing we were under attack and I couldn't find my weapon. Everyone else was scurrying for cover, and I was in the open clearing, yelling out, "Where's my weapon, where's my 16". Finally I remembered where I had put it and low crawled very quickly to it. All of this happened in maybe 20 seconds or so.

My heart was beating fast! We listened and realized we heard no more firing or anything. Then we heard some arguing at one of the guard positions. Two of the guys were arguing with each other and we began to realize some accident must have happened. We all got up to investigate what had caused this debacle.

What we discovered was that at one of the M-60 machine gun positions, the green towel that we always used to covered the gun to keep out the dust and dirt, had partially either blown off the gun or was misplaced on it. This resulted in half or more of the towel falling over a claymore firing device. When one of the guys was walking over to check the gun position he couldn't see the firing device and stepped on it, blowing the claymore. A claymore has a pound and a half of C-4 explosive in it, and going off on a quiet day really wakes you up.

Fortunately no one was hurt, and after we cooled down the two who were arguing, we all checked out the perimeter to make sure no enemy was given our position by the explosion. Then the five of us sat back down and related how that had freaked us all out.

I know we had been stoned, but that explosion brought us all out of it quickly. My heart was still beating a little faster than normal and I just said, "That's it, no more dope in the boonies for me! I absolutely freaked out when the sudden explosion happened and I couldn't find my weapon. If we had been under attack, I might have been killed trying to find my rifle which is never more than a couple of feet from me", I ranted.

"Yeah, that was freaky", chimed in another. "I had my weapon in my hand but the suddenness of that explosion in that simply quiet air and peaceful atmosphere scared me to death", he said.

In any case, I had learned my lesson that day and became thankful for such an experience happening in a safe place instead of somewhere I might have been hurt or killed. I decided that for me there would be no getting high of any kind except on stand-downs or fire-base duty, if at all. That had really shaken me. I stuck with my resolve in the jungle, but had some other times on fire-bases when off duty, and in the rear base camp during stand-downs where I would partake of a joint or two. In the rear getting high was much more beer related than dope for many of us. Doc Shenk

Chilling out in Camp Eagle by just sitting around and talking about home, having a beer or two, and happy to have a rest. Joe Russo, Jim Henson, Dick, and Lt. Hubbard

and SSG. Johnson became drinking buddies with me while in the rear area, and thankfully we were only there once in a while because we always had too much.

A number of the guys on regular duty in rear jobs fixed their hooch's up like the hippies or long hair college students back home. They had many of the same posters of Rock stars and music festivals on their wall dividers, and had great stereo's playing the latest acid rock and Motown tunes. There were times I'd hook up with one of our guys from combat who got a rear job, and we'd just party away the night listening to the great music from home while getting high on pot or beer, or both, doing our best to forget what was going on around us.

Drugs were far too easy to get in Vietnam, and some amphetamines were readily available in the local town pharmacy. What was really a sad thing was that many didn't stick with the pot, but went and bought the addictive drugs, which were also easy to obtain. Opium, heroine, and the like were available, and many became seriously addicted to them, causing great problems for their units.

Soldiers not showing up for duty in the rear areas due to drug usage became a continuing problem, especially in the critical MOS's. Treating these addictions became a real dilemma, and of course many were drummed out of the service with a dishonorable discharge, bringing shame to them when going home, and causing them to continue to stay high to avoid dealing with their problem and facing the shame. It was a very sad situation for many.

The drinkers didn't always just drink beer, but some of the beer they drank contained much higher alcohol content than American beers, which would get them loaded much faster. Then of course there were packages sent from home by friends and family, containing various liquor's they stockpiled, both to drink and sell. The boredom of the off duty hours in rear areas caused a lot of harm to our brothers.

CHAPTER ELEVEN

OPERATIONS FOR A BODY COUNT

I suppose all wars are finally about killing a larger number of the enemy than your own losses. Vietnam was no different, but I was astounded to see such a focus on an every action body count. Not only were many of our officers obsessed with these numbers, they often exaggerated, sometimes greatly, the numbers of enemy killed in a combat action. Many times we were sent on patrols with the CO's final words being, "Get me a body count".

I know for a fact that the numbers of enemy killed reported to the American people are just not believable. It is very true that we killed a huge number more of the enemy than they us, so much so that there was never any need to blow up those numbers, but it was done anyway.

One day our squad was sent out on a patrol, and we made brief contact, probably with a couple of Viet Cong trail watchers. We fired up the area and moved forward trying to find them, but did not. The CO was livid we did not have a "Body Count" for him. "Now you move that squad out further and kill those little bastards, and get me a body count", was his radio call to us.

We moved out as commanded but reluctantly, and after a few more hundred yards we came upon three relatively old shallow graves in the jungle, obviously not from anytime recently. We called in to the CO to report the graves, making sure he knew that they were old and not new, but that made no difference to him. "You men dig up those graves and get me a body count, over" was his reply. We couldn't believe it, but it shouldn't have been a surprise with this "Body Count" mentality floating around.

We dug up the first grave and found two gooks, one lying on top of the other, and a skull separated from the body. One of the guys put it on a stick for a picture, which seems gruesome now, but then death was all around us and we had a different mindset.

Gruesome duty on the CO's orders to get him a body count. We reported three graves we came upon in the jungle and he told us to dig them up. Dick, John Ridgeway, Nelson Reyes, and Tom Brennan

We decided to not to dig up the other graves, and called into the CO that there were two bodies in each grave, and he was happy for his body count of six.

Living in the jungle was a mixed bag of ups and downs.

Many parts of the jungle in the mountainous areas of northern South Vietnam were absolutely beautiful. Breaking out of thick jungle into a crystal clear pool of water, and even once in a great while with a cascading waterfall hundreds of feet above us could be breathtaking.

We would joyfully take advantage of such areas to get clean and cool off. We would be lucky to get a shower in a thirty to sixty day period, and we tried to make the most of any stream we came upon to bathe, or at least quickly wash up, depending on the security of the AO we were in.

Back home on hot days most people would love to be in a swimming pool to cool off. Here in the jungle we were in extremely hot temperatures months on end with little chance to bathe or clean up, much less to swim and have some fun. Even the "Blue Lines" shown on our maps indicating rivers or streams couldn't be trusted in the hot season, as they would dry up and just be dry stream beds.

We came around the bend in a trail and in the distance we heard the sound of rushing water. We continued on as always, slow and methodical, but when you heard that beautiful sound of rushing water you knew it meant at least a bath and maybe more, and fresh cool water for our canteens.

This day was one of those times we hit the jackpot. As we continued forward we stopped in awe of what we saw before us. It was a large, crystal clear pool of water that was about one hundred feet across and maybe fifty feet wide. It was partially shaded and partly in the sun. The waterfall at the far end was about twenty feet high where the water was pouring in from the stream above.

We were in a relatively quiet AO and hadn't made any contact with the enemy in days, but we never were sloppy no matter what. Several of the guys took the first watch, spreading out on both sides of the pool, while I and some others striped down and jumped in. Fortunately our joyful noises were pretty much covered by the loud waterfall.

Dick in a river guard position covering some of the guys who were filling canteens and bathing. Dick had filled canteens at his side, and bathed before them

As I lowered myself into that beautifully clear and cool water I thought I had died and gone to heaven. I took a long drink from the water and just fell back floating in happy thought. After a brief dip, we took out our soap bars and finished bathing.

The men on the first watch were trying to be patient while we enjoyed ourselves; then it was their turn. It was a wonderful day, and now it was back on the move again.

One of the creepy things in the jungle was the leeches that were everywhere. In the hot season they were more near the streams, but in the monsoon season they were everywhere. We tried to make sure our boots were bloused all of the time or you would get leech bites. These little creatures were all of two or three inches long, very slender like a thin worm, but could smell our blood. When you sat down, usually on your helmet, you could see them coming for you as they crawled around the ground and on the brush. The answer was "Bug Juice", a term we gave to Army Insect Repellant; Army Issue Type II A, which when squirted on leach's would make them writhe in pain until dead.

One day while operating in a hot (enemy activity) AO, we climbed up on a high summit to set up an NDP and rest for the night. In the late evening hours we heard movement to our front coming up the hill, and immediately the call went out for artillery. The 105 howitzer rounds came in hitting all around us about one hundred meters from our position. When the "ARTY" stopped, we heard no more movement and felt assured there would be a body count when we left in the morning.

We got up at first light and wanted to sneak out from our position on that hill quietly, because we knew the enemy was now aware of us being there. We weren't even interested in looking for dead enemy to give the CO his body count, because we felt time was of the essence to get out of there before we were attacked again by a larger force.

SSG. Johnson took the point as we headed out, and I walked his slack to cover him. We came to a large tree the artillery had blown down in the night that was lying across the trail we were taking. SSG. Johnson was a short man and had to step up on the trunk and jump over. I was long legged and began to straddle the tree when all of a sudden, "Mac – stop" SSG. Johnson said in a loud whisper. He motioned to me by pointing down in front of me.

I slowly looked down and saw a Krait coiled up and facing my crotch from about 5 inches away. A Krait is a deadly poisonous snake and I froze in place. I couldn't shoot it because that would give away our position. Thinking quickly as he always did, SSG. Johnson moved slowly and slid my large knife out of the leg sheath which was strapped to my other leg, and then quickly moved around behind the snake and tapped on the log behind it. The snake

Dick & SSG. Tom Hunter on the side of a newly "blown" LZ for resupply. They were joking about Dick almost losing the family jewels to a Krait (deadly snake) earlier that morning while crossing a blown-down tree

turned and I rolled out to the other side of the log. It then just slithered off into the jungle, and we continued on. Whew! Later we met up with the rest of the platoon on an LZ in the area awaiting resupply, and SSG. Hunter and I began to joke around about the near miss of my family jewels being destroyed by a snake.

After resupply, we left the LZ and humped a couple of clicks to where we set up our NDP. Our position was in a large area of elephant grass, and we were using machetes' to clear guard positions and sleeping areas. I was standing in the area we had cleared when I felt something go up under the rear of my pants leg fast, then the immense pain. A small centipede, which were venomous got up under my pistol belt and sank its little fangs into my waist. It felt like two white hot needles had just sunk into my skin. I struggled with my pistol belt to get it off and one of the guys killed the centipede. Doc Shenk had to give me some Tetracycline for the poison, but I was all right.

That was my second time for Tetracycline from poisonous bites. A month earlier a new Second Lieutenant was sent out to us, and as we were moving out from the LZ he had landed on he said to me, "Specialist, better put up your long pole antennae". "Right", I said in mocking fashion. "You have a problem obeying orders?" he said in a cocky fashion. "No Sir, but we don't use the long poles in the jungle while walking", I retorted. "Well you do now, put it up", he said.

Frustrated and angry with this "Cherry" Lieutenant, I did what he said. As we started to move out I was having trouble moving as the long-pole kept getting caught in the thick trees. Suddenly something dropped from the tree and hit my shoulder and bit me. I began to burn where I was bitten and then was shaking. I went to the ground and Doc was pulling my rucksack and radio off me. Somebody told me it was a poisonous spider but whatever; I was given Tetracycline and recovered in a few minutes.

I think the LT was embarrassed but I don't ever remember him apologizing for the stupid decision he made. So many officers with no combat experience thought they had to come out and take command without a clue of what they were doing. It was always frustrating when these guys would give orders that were stupid or even dangerous. I always thought that they should have been trained to rely on their Platoon Sergeants until they got their feet wet, but so many wanted to show everyone what leaders they were. It was obvious to us that the real leaders were the ones who conferred with their Sergeants and made decisions based on more information.

That night in our night defensive perimeter I was on my guard duty watch smoking a cigarette in the black darkness. When we smoked, we covered all but our eyes with our poncho liner which hid the burning end of the cigarette from being seen. I remembered how in training my Drill Sergeant would say, "Go ahead and take your chances with smoking at night in the jungle. Charlie loves a lighted target and will aim at the end of your cigarette. However you have to know that Charlie is a bad shot as he will usually hit above the target by two inches". Obviously he meant right between the eyes so I was always careful not to make a target with cigarettes at night.

The typical night in a three man position meant two watch shifts of two hours each. The challenge was to stay awake for each of your two hours, which was often difficult on nights you had been humping the boonies all day. Little things like smoking a cigarette, or using a "Starlight Scope" helped kill the time when all you wanted to do was lie down and go to sleep. Starlight Scopes were only given to us when we were on firebases, and they stayed at the firebase. They were the first of the different night vision equipment that could see in the dark.

If the truth is known, we all fought sleepiness while on guard in the jungle, and once in a while fell asleep. This was a huge danger if we were in a hot AO. It was much easier to stay awake if we knew the enemy was around for fear's sake, than in a quiet AO where we hadn't made contact.

Just then I looked at my watch and saw my guard was over. I crawled over to the poncho hooch to wake Reyes for his watch, and had quite a surprise. He was lying on his back with his eyes wide open and I thought he was dead. When I shook him he woke right up and I was relieved. I found out

Nelson Reyes was a guy who kept us laughing by always joking around. He also slept with his eyes wide open. Freaky!

this was the way Reyes always slept; eyes wide open, and he had big starring eyes that always freaked me out whenever I went to wake him. I'll never know how you can sleep with your eyes wide open, but Nelson Reyes did! Reyes was a funny guy and he always kept us laughing. He would sit on a log at times and as soon as he would notice someone was looking at him he would start wagging his head side to side while turning his head to the right and the left, and did it like he was a mental case and couldn't help it. I'm sure you had to be there, but we all would laugh as it was done with theatrical style.

He used to tick off one of my early squad leaders, Waddell Bishop. Now Bishop would get rattled at Reyes because he was always doing something stupid to try and be funny. For instance, after we would kill a few leaches Reyes would say something like, "Hey Bishop you better call these into the CO for his body count." Or right after Bishop would ream Reyes out for doing something dumb, Reyes would say something like, "Hey Bishop, I can just see it all now when I get back home as Sergeant Nelson Omar Reyes". Bishop would get mad and tell Reyes he would never get above PFC. They were quite funny to watch, and Reyes would always rub it in.

We got the word that the company was being extracted the next morning. For some reason I can't remember, I was acting as our platoon's RTO for that extraction, and the only thing I could think of was that Ed Matajesyk was in the rear already, or maybe he had ETS'd out of the Nam. Anyway we moved to a large field off the side of the jungle that worked well for an LZ because a number of choppers could come in at the same time. There were bushes here and there throughout the field, and the platoon leaders began to move their men to points of landing for the extraction. We were the last platoon to be extracted that day, so LT Morehead and I were coordinating with the choppers.

Now a company size extraction at one time usually took twenty-five to twenty-nine "Slicks" to get everyone out. The officers had been up early listing the men to be on each chopper. We had never had a mistake that I remembered before this day, and there still is a question of whose fault it was, something that never got resolved.

Anyway, the men were lined up in chopper size groups on both sides of the field. The extraction commander came on push, "Delmar One this is Mother Six, over". I answered Mother Six this is Delmar One Alpha, over". Roger Alpha, this is Six, let Delmar One know we are inbound to your location; ETA five mikes, how copy over", the commander said. "Roger Six, I copy ten by ten; when we hear your birds approaching we will pop green smoke at each pick-up point, copy, over". Roger Alpha, I understand we have two pick-up points on either side, is that a Roge?" "That's a Roger Six, and I hear choppers inbound now, we will pop smoke", I said. "Pop smoke on the LZ", LT yelled to the platoon leaders. Two green canisters were popped, one at each LZ point. Delmar One Alpha, this is Six, we acknowledge green smoke, copy", said the commander. "Roger Six", I replied. The choppers were lined up two across with a large interval between them, allowing the time for the men to get on and pull out before the next two came in.

All was going extremely smooth, and LT Morehead said, "Common Dick, let's get to the LZ. We ran around the side of the field from behind the bush we had been observing from. As we got to our pick-up point, the chopper before ours was pulling out, and we began to look up to see ours coming in with one problem; there were no more choppers.

It took us a few seconds to realize we were being left behind. Either we were one bird short or they didn't bring enough. It didn't matter to me, we were being left in the boonies and the enemy may be heading in to check our trash sumps, and I was getting nervous.

My nervousness was not relieved when the LT called to the chopper Commander and told him two of us were left. "What the hell" was his first response, then silence for maybe a minute when he told us to take cover and someone would be back for us, but it might take thirty minutes or so. We ran to one of the bigger bushes in the field and covered each other's back while we lay in the prone position watching out in front of us. We usually would be joking to keep our minds off our situation, but I don't think either of us felt like joking.

The Company Commander came on push and was really hot. Although we were conducting the extraction, I don't believe the LT was responsible for the logistics that were set up to accomplish it. Anyway, I don't know if LT Morehead ever found out, but I didn't, and frankly I didn't care. All we cared about was just getting out of there quickly before Charlie got there to check our sumps!

It was about twenty-five minutes or so when we heard choppers approaching. The Slick they sent for us was accompanied by a Cobra Gunship, just in case. We popped smoke, ran out to the pick-up point, and I think we both were on the chopper before it even landed. Our chopper lifted up and I took a deep breath, thankful we were off to meet the rest of the company.

CHAPTER TWELVE

FRIENDLY FIRE

The worst nightmare I can imagine is being wounded or killed by friendly fire. War is enough of a nightmare without having to worry about your own people hitting you. Unfortunately accidents from weapons of your own troops had been a fact of life of every war, and we could only hope the incidents were few and far between.

Most of us spent little to no time concerned about friendly fire, because we could go nutty thinking about all of the possibilities that could happen. Being accidently shot by someone behind you who forgot to put his safety on, or someone throwing a grenade in triple canopy jungle, only to bounce off a tree he hit accidentally, and have the grenade bounce back into his own men and exploding, were rare but occasional situations in combat. Artillery fire misdirected or called in by miscalculation of the field officer was unfortunately more common, but thankfully not very often.

Even just being careless for a moment could be costly. "Blade 26 this is Bogey 5, over", I called to a chopper that was coming into pick us up on a very narrow finger off the side of a mountain. "Five this is two six, over", came the pilots response. "Two six we have an injury that needs attention", I replied, "Gunshot to the foot", I continued. "Roger, understand you have a gunshot to the foot, over" the pilot said. "Roger two six, waiting instructions, over", I said. After a few seconds of silence, " Roger five, load him on me and we'll get him in. You and the others get on the bird behind me, over". "Roger" I replied.

"Slick" – Huey Helicopter's we rode on most of the time. These were used for combat assaults, medevac's, gun-ships, and resupply most of the time

While we were standing on this narrow finger of the ridge line waiting for the choppers to come in, Reyes had been leaning on his M-16, but had the muzzle on his boot to keep it out of the mud. He had forgotten to put the safety on, and he accidently hit the trigger and blew a hole clear through his boot and foot; right in the middle of an extraction.

I turned around when I heard the shot, and saw his face which indicated he was about to go into shock, and saw the hole in his instep. Shock killed more soldiers than their wounds did, so I immediately began yelling at him and slapping him in the face. 'Reyes you dumb-ass, what the hell's the matter with you", I screamed at him. I was not trying to disparage him for a very painful mistake, but to keep his attention on me to prevent that shock that comes with such things.

As the chopper approached I grabbed Reyes and helped

him get on the bird. He kept telling me, "I'm going to die, going to die". "You're not going to die", I said trying to reassure him. He must not have been convinced because the last time I saw him was when the chopper lifted off the finger LZ, and circled down and around the hill. As the chopper came by me again I could see Reyes in the bird, and I could still hear, "I'm going to die, I'm going to die", as the chopper pulled away. The good news was he made it home and didn't die.

One night in late March 1970, we experienced one of those nightmares. The enemy was attacking at night, and in the dark everything is much more uncertain. When the attack began, Steven Golsh, who everyone called "Bugman" because of his degree in Entomology, was heading for his foxhole. The enemy lobbed a satchel charge in on top of him and he was gone.

The field artillery officer called in an artillery strike to hit the enemy out in front of us. As it came in with the familiar shhhhheww - KABOOM, the shells were hitting the tree tops above some of our positions, and raining down shrapnel on our men. Whether it was the height of the trees above them or short shots was something I guess we'll never know.

"Check your fire...check your fire", was loudly and in a panic screamed into the radio, which meant for the artillery to cease fire immediately. They did so but not before a few previously fired rounds reached us.

Two troops were killed by the friendly fire; John T. Gutekunst, who I had been with earlier in day at the same position, and Louis Barbaria. John was in his foxhole

John Gutekunst Louis Barbaria Steven Golsh

These three brothers were lost the same night and their loss hurt many of us who knew them. Two were killed by friendly fire

but the airburst of the artillery shell exploding over him in the trees rained down shrapnel on him. "Little Joe" Gagliardi was wounded also, and it was a sad night.

"Little" Joe Gagliardi was hit by our friendly fire the night but was ok. This is Joe on FSB Rifle

Previously that day I had been at the same position, but I was called to the CP to take over the company radio while Ed Matejesyk, the regular CO radio operator was leaving for R&R for a week. It never ceased to amaze me how the Lord or fate if you prefer, seemed to look out for me.

Lt. Morehead, our second platoon leader assembled us for a few words the next morning, then we headed out and had to carry our three guys for three days until we could find a safe place to extract them, and get Little Joe medevac'd. We finally got to an LZ that had been previously blown, and were resupplied while sending our fallen brothers and the wounded in.

Several days later another accident happened, but not friendly fire. The terrain in Northern I Corps was mountainous, jungle encrusted, and many times unbelievably steep. One of the guys slipped while negotiating a very steep fall-off and fell. He was hurt and we weren't near another LZ to Medevac him. The CO decided to have the Medevac come out with a jungle penetrator (a seat on a cable) and drop it into us through the trees to get him out.

"Lieutenant have your men set up a perimeter the best they can on this slope, and prepare the injured troop for extraction on a penetrator", the Captain said to LT. Morehead. "Benzol Puddles One this is Dustoff- Niner over", came the call on the radio from the Medevac pilot. "This is Puddles One, over", answered our CO. "Puddles there is a flat finger off the hill you are on about 30 meters from your location", said the pilot. "Get the troop there and prepare someone to hook him up, over". "Roger that", said the CO, and sent a couple of guys with the injured man.

We were all hoping not to receive any enemy fire while this was going on and things moved ahead, but slowly. The penetrator was let down to the flat spot as the Medevac Chopper hovered. The two guys with him quickly had him hooked up and waved at the chopper to bring him up.

CO and Lt Morehead talking to the Medevac pilot about where to drop the jungle penetrator to pick up the injured trooper. After he was on the penetrator the injured man was lifted by cable to the Medevac chopper, and luckily received no enemy fire on the way up

Shortly after this operation, Lt Morehead took a rear job with HHC Company in Camp Eagle, and Our CO went to Battalion HQ. The CO was at the CP on FSB Rifle when it was overrun with sappers, and nearly killed as they threw satchel charges into the CP bunker while he was in there.

Lt Morehead, after surviving jungle operations for a number of months, was in a jeep when it hit a land mine throwing him about twenty-five feet from the jeep, and critically wounding the Jeep driver. Most of us were quite surprised because we always thought a rear job or even one on a firebase would be safer than in the boonies.

After this operation we were extracted to another FSB to secure for a few days until we were given the next operational assignment. After setting up on the firebase, we were sitting around killing some time cleaning weapons and shooting the breeze. The choppers had left our mail when they dropped us off, and after reading my letters I sat down with the latest Stars & Stripes military paper to see what was going on in the world.

"You have got to be kidding me", I shouted so others could hear me. Several of the guys huddled around to see

Another resupply coming in. See the red mail bag corner above the tree. Mail was always in red bags and one of the most sought after items in any resupply

what I was talking about. There on the front page was a picture of a student who had been shot by National Guardsmen at Kent State in Ohio. "What in the hell is the matter with them shooting students; I can't believe this", I exclaimed. "This world is surely going to hell", I continued. "Why would they shoot unarmed students; are they just crazy back home? I asked. "If they want to kill someone, send those dumb asses here and they can go for it, but college kids, what is the matter with this world"? We discussed this news story for quite some time, but finally had to get back to the tasks at hand.

The Kent State shootings stayed with me for a few days as I could honestly not think of a reason for anyone to shoot unarmed civilians, and college kids at that. Now I know many college students were pushing the limits with all of their protesting crap, and even taking over campuses, but they were peaceful demonstrations from what I had heard, and why would you shoot into that?

Friendly Fire incidents were always heart wrenching to me, and they seemed so wrong, but in a war and especially combat, things are so harried that you sometimes wonder how anyone made it out. Fortunately, I witnessed very few friendly fire incidents, but those I saw were very hurtful. Of course there were other non-combat injuries that were caused by the terrain we operated in, which were just as painful when they happened to someone.

One such incident in our Company happened in another platoon from ours where one of our guys became paralyzed from another bad fall off the side of a cliff. We were in a hot AO and when the medics got to him he couldn't move from the waist down. The CO called for a Medevac with another jungle penetrator, but this one had to be what we called a basket.

The chopper arrived and was hovering over the spot where the man lay, and lowered the basket through the trees to the medics below. They managed to get our guy in the basket, laid down and strapped in, but fortunately leaving his arms outside of the straps.

The medics gave the thumbs-up to the cable man on the chopper, and they began raising him to the chopper some fifty-five feet or so above. He was about two thirds of the way up when pow…pow…pow…pow…pow, an enemy machine gun opened up on them. The tracers were first going over and under the basket and our guy was freaking out about being hit while he lay helplessly. The basket continued to be pulled up by the medevac crew, but under fire it moves far too slowly.

Our guy began motioning with his hands to pull it up faster, but of course they were pulling him up as fast as they could. The gooks then turned the machine gun on the chopper and began hitting it. The SOP for this situation is clear; if the medevac is in danger for being shot down and taking everyone with it, the cable man at the door of the chopper is to cut the cable and release the penetrator while the chopper then pulls out to save the aircraft and crew.

Now the basket was almost to the chopper and was still being pulled up when the order was given to the door man. Bullets were now hitting the chopper and the pilots had to try and save the aircraft and crew. Our guy saw the door man with the cable cutters, and just as he was about to cut the cable, our guy was up to the skid. He wrapped his arms around that skid with a death grip and yelled at the door man to get out of here.

With that the pilot laid the bird over to the right and away they went, with our guy still holding on for dear life to that chopper skid. They all made it but what a tense situation; waiting for the bullets to hit you while being helpless to take cover, then looking up to see they were going to cut the cable which would cause you to drop over fifty feet to your death strapped in a basket.

Back in the rear sometime later, our trooper had recovered and was waiting to be released for combat duty. We sat in the orderly room as he related the story and his unbearable fear of being cut from the medevac and falling to his death. He also laughed and joked about the situation, and his grabbing onto the chopper skid so tight that he knew he would make it. Thank you Lord!

We moved to a firebase which was not like most up on top of a hill, but was on low ground and could have been harder to defend if we had been attacked. We had no enemy attack those few days that we were there, and then we were told some great news. We were ordered to prepare for the stand-down of stand-down's meaning the 101st Airborne – Eagle Beach.

Everyone was eager to get extracted from the firebase, but found out we were walking out rather than flying. We had to get everything ready quickly and the mortar platoon commander made the decision to have his mortar guy's fire up all of the existing ammo rather than hump them out, which would have been difficult. They were really firing up the rounds of mortars much too fast, and once again an accident that was costly occurred.

This is a similar mortar pit to the one the man had his fingers blown off and his eye blown out.

I was standing about ten meters from one of the mortar pits with second platoon SSG. Johnson. We were in front of a wall to a hooch packing our ruck sacks when all of a sudden, Ka-Boom, a loud explosion behind us happened and ffff-tttttt, the sound of shrapnel hit all around us. I looked at the wall and could literally see shrapnel that had gone right by us and stuck in the wall.

We immediately hit the ground expecting we were taking incoming rounds. We then heard the cry from the men in the pit behind us who were wounded badly, and SSG. Johnson said "Common Mac, Hurry", and we went running to them and jumped into the pit.

It turns out these guys were feeding the mortar tubes from both sides of the mortar. First one fed and shot, then another fed and shot. Unfortunately they lost their timing in hurrying and one of them was feeding the tube before the other round got out. It came out and exploded, blowing off most of the hand of the guy feeding last, and injuring everyone in the pit. They were lucky they weren't killed, and we were lucky we weren't killed from all the shrapnel hitting around us.

The man that had his hand blown off also was hit in one of his eyes. SSG. Johnson calmly told me, "Mac put a dressing over his eyes", so he couldn't see what had happened to his hand, but it was too late. I covered his eyes but he said immediately, "I saw it...I saw it my hand is gone", he cried out. By this time medics were there and taking over. SSG. Johnson had managed to stop the bleeding of the blown off hand which may have saved this guy's life. His fingers were still bouncing around on the ground.

SSG. Lonnie Johnson in the Boonies with his map. He was one of the best fighter's I ever knew and someone you wanted with you in a firefight. When the man had his hand blown off and his eye out, he was quick to instruct me how to help him while he worked on keeping him out of shock, the biggest killer in the war

As we started to walk away, their CO came running to see what had happened, and the guy we helped started yelling at him for making them move so fast to get rid of the mortar shells. A more heartbreaking fact was that today was supposed to be this troopers last day in Nam, but he had extended his tour of duty for two months to get the early out of the Army offered to those who would extend their tours for a couple of more months. Many had seven to twelve months left to serve when they went home, and making this extension in Nam would erase the rest and they would then be discharged right from Vietnam. I had seven months left in the States when I got home, but this catastrophe insured I would never extend my tour of duty.

CHAPTER THIRTEEN

EAGLE BEACH

Except for the very lucky few who managed to get there a second time during their tour, the best thing in the Nam other than R&R, was a couple of days at Eagle Beach. This was the 101st's beach resort of sorts, and a time of just rest, relaxation, swimming, sunning, and eating. The choppers would extract us out of the boonies and land us right on the beach. We would be dirty, weapons hanging all over us, our ruck sacks and the like, but once there it all changed for the good.

Dick in forefront and the guys land on Eagle Beach for a great stand-down only experienced once in a year by most Screaming Eagles

Not even CSM Sabalauski was there to harass us. We were free, after turning in weapons, to do whatever our little hearts desired. The bar was open, hot chow ready, hot showers available, clean clothes laid out, and nothing but time to enjoy.

Eagle Beach was located on a stretch of sandy beach on the South China Sea. There were quite a number of wooden buildings erected for sleeping quarters, dining hall, bar, game room, and a more quite day room for just relaxing and enjoying the absence of combat and humping those rucks. Many caught up on their letters home, or lay on the beach drinking beer, while others swam in the oceans clean salt water. I remember having some jungle rot on my leg and hand that started from scratches of some "wait-a-minute" vines in the boonies. A small scratch in the jungle can quickly open up and get green and very ugly from all of the bacteria and sweat. The salt water at Eagle Beach cleaned and healed up my problems very quickly.

Wait-a-minute vines were all over the jungle and we tried to avoid them whenever possible. You could be walking along a trail or cutting your way through with a machete' and be stopped dead by these little annoying vines. It seemed like they were attracted to you like a magnet and could literally grab you anywhere. I had one just come at me like it intended to and hook on my eyelid as I was moving. My eyelid must have stretched out inches and I stopped in pain immediately, Then you'd have to unhook yourself just like from a fishhook. They had barbed stickers all over them and if you got entangled in them you'd have to cut your way out.

When we were on a Firebase or enjoying a stand-down like Eagle Beach, there was usually a poker game going on in the evenings. Many times SSG. Johnson and I were asked to play by some of the officers, and for me this was a lot of fun. Money had little importance in combat, so it wasn't about the money. It was a time of sharing who we were over a friendly game of stud poker, or perhaps blackjack. It always seemed refreshing to me to listen and hear how our officers were very much like the rest of us. You didn't usually know much about the officers because they were not supposed to fraternize with the troops, so this was a pleasant change when everyone sort of let their hair down.

"Hit me" I said to the company commander who was the blackjack dealer in the game we were playing at the time. I received the five of hearts which brought my total to twenty. I bet five dollars on the twenty and the dealer flipped over an ace, giving him twenty-one. "Sorry Dick" Captain Faulkenberry said, "Twenty-one". Thank God it was dealers' choice and the next game was seven card stud; my favorite. I usually did well in poker games in the Army with the exception of Black-jack.

One night a number of my buddies and I were out on the beach late. It was quite dark, but still enough moonlight to see somewhat. We were drinking and talking of home, and just enjoying the peace with the sound of the waves coming in and a pleasant breeze blowing in off the water. We went swimming and for the first time I saw phosphorescent plankton light up in the water from the moonlight as we swam.

The next morning a couple of the fellas and I decided to go to church, and we walked out from the beach to a beach road. "This feels weird", John said as we walked along this road. "I know", I said agreeing but not sure why. It then hit us. "We don't have any weapons", someone said, as they had been turned in at the "resort". That was probably the first time for any of us to be out without weapons except when in Camp Eagle.

Once we were back from church, we went back on the beach where games of football or Frisbee throwing were going on. While participating with the guys, my mind went back to days on the beach at home, and all of the fun we would have. The group of friends I hung around with after graduating high school, were classmates home for the summer from college. We all had motorcycles of one kind or another, and it was doubly fun to ride as a group to the beach and back.

After being at Eagle Beach most of us felt well rested and thankful we had the time to just re-gather our thoughts. It was amazing what a few days of R&R could do for the psyche'. Once we got all packed up and back in jungle fatigues, our thoughts turned toward what we might be heading into in the upcoming days. The paved chopper pads were on the beach and as our chopper lifted off and out over the water, and I took one last look at a great place I would not see again.

From Eagle Beach we were taken to an old abandoned Fire Base where we would set up a temporary FSB to cover some of the Battalion in the jungle around it. My platoon was selected to go out in the morning and recon the area surrounding the firebase, and we were to go out about two clicks in several directions.

That evening we heard the popping of enemy tubes and were scattering trying to find a hole. A couple of the guys, as usual, were standing on the edge of the hill looking out to see if they could spot the enemy. They had a good idea where the firing was coming from, and we only received a few rounds being happy nobody was hurt.

A LOH chopper (a small copter we called a Loach) came

on push and asked for the direction of the enemy firing. We told him and he flew out in front of us, and had mounted on that little chopper a mini-gun, and a grenade launcher. I had not seen that equipment on that small of a bird before, and probably for good reason. As he moved in on the adjacent hill across from us, he fired his mini-gun first. The firing literally pushed the chopper back in the air with each burst. Then he opened up with his automatic grenade launcher, and thump, thump, thump, thump, thump, maybe twenty times firing grenades that were on a belt like machine gun ammo. Then, boom, boom, boom, boom, boom, as we watched the area get covered with shrapnel from the

Richard Hayman with a LOH chopper we called a Loach. These were used many times by Battalion Commanders who would fly over battle scenes attempting to direct our firing movements. When used by higher up's in these situations they were referred to as Charlie-Charlie Birds, or Command and Control choppers

grenades. This was quite impressive until an F-4 Phantom jet came on push.

"Razor 5, Razor 5, this is Smoke-Bringer 26, over", came

the call from the pilot. "I'm going in and spraying the area with my Vulcans (Vulcan Cannons), which were the M-61 20 mm Gatling machine guns on the jet that fired and sounded like a min-gun. All of the bullets had exploding heads on them and could blow a body apart quickly. It was dusk when the jet rolled in, and he opened up with the r-r-r-r-r-r-r-r-r-r-r-r-roar of the Vulcan cannons, which had large exploding heads. In the near dark we could see the thousands of mini explosions all over the area as he made his run. It was something to behold, unless you were a gook on the wrong end of the firing. "Razor 5, Smoke-Bringer heading out, over", said the pilot. "Thanks man", said our Lt., and off he went.

The next morning we went out on patrol and humped all day looking for the enemy. As it was nearing twilight that evening, we were on top of a ridge line looking down at a large open field hundreds of meters away. There were two bushes in the middle of that field, and someone said, "Hey, there are a couple of gooks out there". Now it was getting dark but I could easily tell they were bushes. Several of us got together on the edge of the ridge line, and one of the guys said, "I think we need to call for a few "fire-cracker" rounds to take care of the enemy in the open".

"Fire-Cracker" rounds were supposed artillery shells that had been developed for large numbers of enemy in the open, and we had never seen them. We even had been told they did not exist, and were against the Geneva Convention. They were supposed to be an artillery round filled with numerous small grenade balls, that when hitting the ground, a pre-explosion blew the balls into the air, then they all went off throwing shrapnel everywhere.

We decided that what could we lose? "Fire-mission, Fire

mission, enemy in the open, coordinates Bravo-26, Hotel -12", began our call. "Requesting Fire-cracker rounds, fire for effect, over", and we then waited for a response. To our surprise, there was no response. We heard the artillery firing way off in the distance, and we waited to see what we would get. Then, in they came with a s-h-h-h-h-h-hah, Bump. Then a louder boom, then boom, boom, boom, boom, boom, boom as the little grenades all exploded at once filling the air with brightly burning shrapnel easily seen in the dark.

"Well, I guess we have "Fire-cracker" rounds" someone said. We called into the Arty guys, "Redleg two-niner, you got 'em, you got 'em" we told them, giving them some ridiculous body-count, and feeling quite proud of ourselves that we had put an end to the myth.

The next day we stopped for a break, and decided to have some lunch. I pulled out a can of Beans & Franks and began to eat. "Hey, I can taste this", I said in amazement as I had not tasted anything for almost a year and a half due to the brain injury I had back home after a fight. "Big deal", came the response from one of my buddy's, "You were better off before not tasting this C-ration junk"! Well he may have felt that way, but I was ecstatic to be able to taste again.

As always our tongue-in-cheek humor was a regular thing with us because it helped us to laugh and relieve stress. A day earlier I was sitting on my Steele Pot (helmet) and looking at a Stars and Stripes paper when something dawned on me. "Hey, what day is it", I said to the others with me. Someone said, "May first". "Hey, I'm twenty-one years old today", I exclaimed, to which several came right back with, "Big deal, you won't live to be twenty-two"! Fortunately, they were wrong.

It did seem strange that most of us were in our very low twenties or younger. There was a guy in one of the other platoons who lied about his age at 16 to get into the Army, and was now 17. They called him Junior, and he looked more like a blonde haired fourteen year-old. So many young men in the prime of life being sent to a war zone and putting it all on the line seemed wrong to me, but I understood that it takes young, healthy men to fight wars.

Helicopters came to pick us up and took us out to a fire base precariously close to the A Shau Valley. The A Shau Valley was a place that when mentioned, would bring chills to our spines. It had been a place of horrific battles and great carnage that no one ever wanted to go to, and was clearly labeled, "the valley of the shadow of death".

From there we began a company size search and destroy mission just east of the valley, and we were all wondering if this mission was going to lead us into this fearful place. One of the reasons the A Shau was so dangerous was that it was one of the key entry points into South Vietnam for men and weapons brought along the Ho Chi Minh Trail by the North Vietnamese Army.

One big mistake we were making was that GI's, being lazy, we decided to move down a "Red Ball" (wide trail or road cut through the jungle). We knew it was always better to cut our way through the brush to avoid booby-traps, but it was also a lot more work, and much slower. It was very hot as usual, and there was an eerie feeling walking down a road so close to the A Shau Valley out in the open like that. I kept thinking we were making a mistake by walking in the open in a hot AO, but I had to admit it was a lot easier than cutting our way through the jungle. Fortunately, we did not run into the enemy, but that feeling of danger was still permeating the air.

We made our way to the objective, and much to our surprise, found an abandoned enemy bunker complex. That was a relief due to what we expected to find. The officers got together with our artillery officer to mark the coordinates of the bunkers, and they would later have a fire mission or two on those coordinates in hopes of catching the enemy unexpectedly. A number of us in the meantime carefully walked through the bunker-complex to check for anything of value that may have been left behind. We found nothing except some clothing and other odds and ends.

We started back, and being doubly stupid, went back the same way. Heading back the same way we had come, in any area especially anywhere near the A Shau where there was a much bigger chance of NVA trail-watchers, was very dangerous. For one reason, small booby-traps could be set up quickly to cause injuries and possibly killings, and the enemy could use small mortars that they could instantly set up farther ahead on the road we were moving down.

My platoon had the point position on the return trip. The Lieutenant Lippy asked me to walk point on one side of the road, and assigned someone else the other side. Walking point was not something I relished doing, but for some reason they never asked me if I wanted to do things or not.

We had been moving about thirty minutes when the LT called up to me and said, "OK Dick, pull off the road and take five". I had moved out into the road a little when the

LT was calling me to tell me to pull off. As I turned to the right, I stepped over a planted enemy anti-tank mine missing it by inches. I couldn't see it because the road was very muddy, and left no sign of any earth disturbance. I walked over about fifteen or twenty feet off the road, and began taking my ruck sack off. Lieutenant Lippy and his RTO (radio operator) were making their way up to my location. LT Lippy also managed to step over the mine, but his RTO was not as lucky.

I was just sitting down on top of my ruck when, "KA-BOOM", a terrific blast occurred. Shrapnel hit all around me, but didn't touch me. I looked into the air as I was being blown down by the blast, and saw Lt. Lippy approximately ten feet in the air in a vertical position. Just as I looked at him, his pants blew off in mid-air from the concussion. He was blown up that high in the air and was seven feet or so in front of the guy who hit it. I watched as he came back down hitting the ground with a thud in the mud. Just after he hit, what was left of his RTO came down right in front of me, with pieces of his body showering down over all of us. The man who hit the mine was just a torso with no arms or legs. His head was still attached, but no face was left.

There was dead silence, and I could see across the road that several of my buddies on the other side had been hit by the shrapnel, and were bleeding. LT Lippy began to moan in the middle of the road, and I could see blood from shrapnel wounds all over him. I grabbed my large field dressing and without thinking, began to run to LT Lippy.

"Dick...Dick...stop man...stop....minefield", Willie Thomas one of my wounded buddies from the other side of the road yelled at me as I got about half way to the LT. I then began to panic. Not realizing the potential danger, and wanting to get to the wounded LT fast, I had just run into what could be a minefield. I stopped and began to look around me for any sign of mines, but couldn't tell as it was all mud. A couple of my buddies began to slowly inch their way on their stomachs to LT Lippy and me with bayonets probing for mines.

As I stood there trying to be extremely still, I began to think of what could have happened to me if I had hit another one. It is times like this when your mortality spins throughout your mind, and being this close to death could make you flip out if you let it. It was calming to have buddies coming to get you with words of, "Don't worry, we got ya", and other reassuring words reminding me that I was not alone.

Finally, a trail was cleared to us, and LT Lippy and the other wounded guys were medevac'd, while a number of us walked around picking up the body pieces of his radio operator. "Just another day in the Nam", one of the guys said, to which we all mumbled,"Yeah". We all knew this was not just another day in the Nam for the man blown up, his family, or LT Lippy and the other wounded. It was a day that would change their lives dramatically. Maybe the worst part of wounds and deaths in a war is the fact that you feel you're glad it was someone else and not you.

The gruesome task of finding all of the pieces of this man's body and putting them into a body bag was very difficult. His body parts were literally all over the place and it took us about a half of an hour to feel we had most of him with us. In the meantime we were aware that our position had been compromised by the explosion, but no one was willing to leave our brother or his body parts behind. Of course as standard SOP we had men out in front of us in a large perimeter watching for enemy coming our way during this body recovery.

We were all extremely glad to get to the LZ for our extraction out of this area and depressing day. Little did we know we were about to go into a much worse area, and begin a fight on two different mountains that we would never forget.

CHAPTER FOURTEEN

COMBAT ASSAULT

I had made a number of CA's in my time with the company, but none as frightening as the one into Hill 882. We had been operating in a hot AO near the A Shau Valley, an NVA (North Vietnam Army) stronghold on Hill 714.

This is a good depiction of an open area CA (Combat Assault). Many times the men jumped out five or more feet off the ground to get out and start running if it were a hot LZ

We were on Hill 714 where we had been for a number of days. While many units were in fierce major confrontations with the NVA on Hill 714, we were running patrols and hitting patches of NVA with brief firefights. We had a dog unit come out with us with two dogs and handlers, and were interesting to watch.

The dogs were German Shepherds and very well trained which is what surprised me with what happened one night. We were set up in our NDP and I had just come off guard. It was very dark as usual, but you could see very weak shadows of movement so the stars may have been bright that night. I had just fallen asleep when those two dogs started viciously barking in the dark. I grabbed my rifle and sat up quickly. I could hear all kinds of movement but couldn't see much of anything.

I was completely scared and heard the trainer settling down the dogs. I don't think they ever knew what set those dogs off that night, but I had been afraid that all of the barking was giving our position away in a very bad place. Anyway, we all got through the night but pretty sleepless, and off we went again the next day.

Handler, Dog, and Tom Brennan. From time to time the trained dogs would be brought out to try and sniff out the enemy and give us early warning.

There were times we would find tunnel complexes that were unbelievably elaborate. The North Vietnamese had been digging these out all over Southern Vietnam since the war with the French, and had obviously improved them over the years that they were fighting us. Some of these tunnel complexes were way below ground and dug into a mountain. The deep ones were bomb proof because they were many feet below the surface dug right out of the mountain rock.

The more elaborate ones had multiple camouflaged entrances and exits, and contained meeting and planning rooms, sleeping areas for a large numbers of soldiers, and hospital rooms with lighting for operations and treating their wounded. These tunnel complexes ran underground for great distances and were literally impossible to spot from the air. Ground troops would sometimes stumble on them by noticing either a hastily covered opening or observe gooks going in or coming out by chance. Some had been found in the French war and made note of, and were checked out if we were in the area to see if they had been reopened.

There were also small tunnels, some of which were not dug too deep but offered shelter to enemy troops as they traveled down the Ho Chi Minh Trail, carrying supplies and ammo from the North. These smaller tunnels were easier to destroy but the large complexes were virtually indestructible.

When a tunnel was discovered, each unit had small men who were designated "Tunnel Rats" to go in them and scope out the situation. This was a dangerous and of course confining job, and they had to be slow, methodical, and very observant. They took a pistol and a flashlight into very dark and scary situations. The entrances were the first obstacles, which many times were booby-trapped with trip grenades, and even poisonous snakes. Other times there was a ledge dug off to the side of the dark entrance where an enemy soldier would be positioned to either stab or shoot the first to come in, then run away into the complex fast before a grenade was thrown in to get him.

One of our units had a tunnel rat begin to enter a tunnel and the outside guys were holding his feet to pull him out quickly if something happened. They felt him go limp and yanked his boots pulling him out. As usual, a grenade was quickly thrown in to kill anyone or anything that might have been there. It turns out in this case that our guy began his entrance in the dark opening, and bringing his flashlight up from his side turned it on right in the face of a gook only inches from him. He actually fainted going limp and as they pulled him out, and the gook must have di di mau'd fast because the grenade didn't get him

Before entering these tunnels and complexes it was always smart in my opinion, to throw in the grenade first before entering. This seems like common sense that would take care of any surprises in the opening, but if it looked like an active location, the officers would prefer the element of surprise to possibly capture some enemy for information about other locations of complexes. Tunnel Rats were very brave and maybe a little nutty.

Bunker complexes were a little different. The old WWII bunkers were generally above ground or dug into the hill elevated enough to see and have a field of fire. In Vietnam many bunkers were level with the ground and we wouldn't realize we were in the midst of one until someone spotted an opening, or the enemy opened up on us. They would use many of these below ground bunkers to store weapons, rockets, and food, and to ambush any passing troops in the area. These were easier to blow, but usually still left holes in the ground that they would just come to and re-camouflage the tops. Blowing up their food and weapons was a triumph for us because the the only way they could get the weapons to the South was to physically carry them for many miles from the North.

Another danger in these flat bunker complexes, were the "Spider Holes". Among and around many of these complexes were spider holes, which were shallow small pits, covered by a camouflaged pop-up trap door. The enemy would wait until our unit was in or very near the complex, and pop-up, shoot a soldier and drop back down under the trap door before we could see them.

Fortunately for us most of these spider holes were not a part of a tunnel system so once the gooks got in them they had to stay there until we found them or we were gone. Usually we would hit the ground and everyone just waited for the next one to pop up, then we would pop them. If we felt we had entered a massive complex, we would call in the Phantoms to bomb the area and napalm the complex.

Army Intelligence (sometimes an oxymoron), had identified an NVA regiment stronghold dug into another mountain we called Hill 882, and our "Higher-ups" decided we needed to take that hill. As we did almost every four days to get resupplied, we had to blow an LZ (landing zone) at a level spot of the hill we were on, to allow choppers to extract us off of that hill and CA us to Hill 882. We were all told what lay ahead of us, and tried to ignore the fear we had for the battle that was coming.

For some unknown reason, probably the luck of the draw, I had gone into the last couple of CA's on the first bird. If the LZ is hot, then the first bird is the chopper that gets all the fire by being the forward probe into the CA. Fortunately, both of those ended up not being a hot LZ, and so landing without incident I was very thankful.

Richard Hayman talking to the chopper pilot coming into an LZ, and giving the all clear.

This early day in May 1970, I was put on the second chopper, which meant if the first chopper received fire, all others would pull out until the Cobra Gunships would saturate the LZ with mini-guns and rockets to clear it for a more secure combat assault. By being on the second bird you weren't supposed to go into a hot LZ. As fate had it, we were approaching Hill 882, and I was hanging out of the left door of the second chopper watching the first bird approach. The side doors of all of the choppers were wide open so we could get out fast and hit the ground running. As the first chopper began to go in, it was peppered with small arms fire, and red smoke grenades were dropped out of both of its doors as it pulled out indicating hot LZ – don't go in.

I was relieved but only briefly as the pilot turned to me at the door and said, "We're going in". I couldn't believe my ears until I was jarred back to reality as two Cobra gunships came right past our two doors on either side firing rockets and mini-guns with mind deafening noise. The Cobras were so close to us I felt I could almost reach out and touch the pilots.

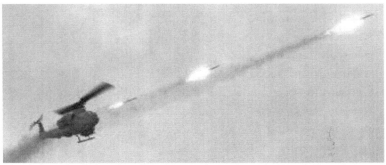

Good shot of a Cobra Gun Ship firing rockets at an enemy position. Cobras were instrumental in clearing LZ's during combat assaults, and for close-in support when we were pinned down or needed extra fire power

Once again I'm going in on the first bird, but this time into a hot LZ. Fortunately in these fear stricken moments, my training would take over and off I'd go. The chopper was not about to land in this hot LZ's because they need to be in and out quickly to avoid being shot down. The pilots took us in and we were hanging out both sides of the doors so we could quickly jump out and run for cover. Going in fast they got within 5 feet of the ground as we jumped out while they were still moving.

I don't remember running any faster in my life, firing my M-16 as I went and jumping behind a blown down tree for cover. Lt. Richardson, our platoon leader came in right behind me, and we fired till we heard the enemy had stopped. LT ordered my squad to secure the LZ as the others came in, and the next squad headed out down a trail to recon the area. They had not gone far when we heard the

AK-47's open up on them. The enemy had been forced off of the LZ and had moved a couple of hundred meters off of the LZ to avoid the Cobra's firing on them, and to ambush the first of our unit to head their way.

Two of our men were killed in that ambush and a couple more were wounded. SFC. Manning, our Field First Sergeant was with those men as they ran into the ambush. One of the enemy figured out he was the leader and jumped up firing point blank at his head. The bullet hit SFC. Manning's helmet and ricocheted off hitting Peter Nolan in the throat and killing him. Another of our men was hit by the ensuing firing and also killed.

This point squad managed to kill a number of the enemy in the encounter, and caused them to retreat back from our men. They continued to move forward and began setting up a company perimeter. As my squad had been ordered to secure the LZ, we were the guys who had to put our brothers into body bags as they brought them to the LZ for extraction and for medevac'ing the wounded. Little did we know this was the beginning of a huge, multi-battalion fight that would last for two weeks.

Loading a body bag with a still warm comrade, motionless and gone was hard then, and was always hard. We tried to make sure that they had their tags, and their weapons had been brought back with them as we didn't want Charlie to be given anything that could be used against us. Once ready to zip up the bag you would just go numb for a minute as you realized that could be you next time.

The rest of Alpha Company was CA'd into the hill, and we watched diligently out around the LZ to make sure they came in OK. I kept looking at the body bags of the first two to be killed on that hill, and as we guarded their bodies a sense of sadness came over me as I reflected on these two men…these two brothers who had been alive and vibrant just minutes before. The realization that it can happen to anyone at any time in a war zone can be very overwhelming if you let it. It caused me to think of my own mortality, and made me draw close to my savior Jesus the Christ.

As other units of the 101st were CA'd into the LZ, the Phantom Jets had been summoned from the aircraft carriers in the Gulf of Tonkin. We would be calling them numerous times during this ferocious battle to aid us in taking the hill. Throughout that first day we encountered hit and run attacks from NVA soldiers, and with the continuous pounding of our artillery, Cobra Gunships, F-4 jets fighters, and small arms fire fights, I longed for some quiet to get my head together. It didn't come very often, and when it did, you were worried about what might be sneaking up on you.

I personally was very thankful that we had a new Battalion Commander, Lt. Colonel Shay, code name "Shamrock". He had recently replaced the former commander who called himself "Cajun Tiger", and was an incompetent leader in my opinion. When we would make contact with the enemy, no matter how big the force, I was told he refused to call in the F-4 Phantom jets to aid us. He would tell our officers that "You are the 101st Airborne, we don't need the Navy". Now in fairness, I never heard him say that, but while he was in command, I never saw the Navy Pilots called in. Also, Cajun Tiger would ride thousands of feet above a battle in his LOH Charlie-Charlie (command and control) helicopter while giving orders to advance on an enemy entrenched. I used to say to myself, yea, get your cowardly ass down here and we'll see how fast you advance. I didn't like him!

Now Shamrock was a horse of a different color, in that he believed in using all options available to him. So here we were on Hill 882 and facing a huge, entrenched enemy, and Colonel Shay had the Phantoms on push quickly napalming and bombing stronghold positions that would have cost many more lives to take without them. He is what I call a true combat commander.

Setting up that first night our company split into three platoons, each setting up their own NDP's (night defensive perimeters) about 400-500 meters from the other, but all on a small part of one side of the mountain. We dug in and covered our foxholes as best we could. "Mac, get your claymores out there", SSG Johnson said pointing to where he wanted them, "then put your trip- flares out in front of them about 15 feet or so" he continued.

What was funny about him directing me and some of the others was that we had been putting out claymores and trip-flares in many operations, but everyone was just nervous about this situation, and the leaders felt they had to make sure all was covered. He knew he really didn't have to tell us but I think it helped him deal with the stress factor we were all feeling.

The NVA (North Vietnamese Army) were well trained, not at all like the VC (Viet Cong) who usually hit and ran. The NVA would stay and fight until eventually overwhelmed by the superior firepower Americans always brought to the table. They had "Sapper" teams that were trained to find our trip flare wires in the dark and disarm the trip-flares, and then find our claymore mines. One trick of the NVA Sappers was to turn our claymores around toward us, move

Richard Hayman settling in a NDP (Night Defensive Position) while always by his radio on top of his rucksack at his knee

away from them and make noise or purposely blow a trip-flare. GI's are taught to blow their Claymore's immediately when a trip-flare goes off. Now Claymore mines are packed with C-4 plastic explosive behind 700 steel balls that look like small ball-bearings. The mines are directional, so if one was turned around toward our own guys, if they blew the mine it may easily kill our guys instead of the enemy.

One trick I learned was to plant a trip-flare under my claymores, forcing the legs of the claymore down over the trip-flare. If the dirt was hard the legs would hold down the spoon of the trip flare (like a grenade spoon), and I would pull the pin on the trip flare. If the enemy would find the claymore and pull it up to turn it on us, the spoon would fly on the trip flare and the surprised Sapper would be holding the Claymore when it was blown. We usually had to dig a

Claymore Mine   Trip Flare

Part of any NDP was the positioning of Claymore mines out in front of our positions, protected by a trip-wire to a trip-flare a few feet in front of the claymores

small indentation for the trip flare under the Claymore to insure the legs on the claymore would go into the dirt far enough to hold the trip flare's spoon in place when we pulled the pin.

After getting things set up for the night, I decided to heat some water over a heat-tab and make some hot chocolate. "What are we drinking", came the familiar expression from some of the guys who smelled the drink. "Get your cup and have some of this", I said which was my general response. "Guys, I don't think we're going to get much sleep tonight", I continued as we were all wired with fearful anticipation of what was likely to happen. Fortunately that first night pretty much went without incident, other than artillery flares coming over the area periodically, and a few fire missions by our artillery when someone thought they had movement. None of us had much of an idea of what we had gotten ourselves into, but we would soon find out!

The next morning the third squad of our platoon was ordered to move forward and recon the area ahead. Sgt. Stansfield was the squad leader, and he took his men up the trail. They were not gone long when we heard enemy weapons open up on them as they walked into an ambush. The call for help came on the radio, and Lt. Richardson sent the second squad to help them out. As we quickly but carefully headed up the trail, the firing was quite intense. I was scared to death as we moved closer and closer. The exchange of machinegun, rifle, and RPG fire was nerve-racking. Tom Brennan, our squad leader began to shout as we arrived to the scene of mayhem. "Ok, spread out on line…Dick, take the left flank…Jeff right flank…let's get these guys out 'a here". A few of the guys broke left with me, and a few right with Jeff.

We came upon the third squad and they had been shot up pretty badly. We put out a lot of fire with our M-16's, M-60 Machinegun, and M-79 Grenade Launcher. I was hugging the ground as bullets were hitting around us, and lifting my head up to see around some brush. I slapped another magazine into my '16 and as I looked forward I saw an enemy soldier get up on his knees, pull up an RPG looking right at me, and fire. Whoooosh was the sound of the rocket as it barely went over my head and exploded when hitting a tree behind me.

I looked to my left and saw Sgt. David Stansfield who was sitting, leaning up against a tree. I started over to him sort of sliding low on my knees while firing my rifle from under my right arm, and scooting between rifle bursts. I finally reached David and the tree he was up against was huge, offering us some protection from the area the gooks were firing from. His arm had been shot up causing the bone to be broken and sticking out through his skin and blood was flowing. I took my field dressing and began to wrap the wounded arm. It was a mess and I was no medic, but now I realized why the Army spent so much time in training us in all of the critical first aid situations. While I was wrapping up his mutilated arm, I could see something out of my left eye that seemed out of place. I looked up at his face, and instead of cringing in pain, he was smiling at me. I said, "Stan, what's so funny?" He looked at me and said, "Dick, they have to send me home for this one!" I thought for a few seconds about his comment then thought you lucky son of a bitch.

The firing continued and more of our guys came up the trail until the enemy had finally broken off the contact. "Smitty" (Wayne Smith) the third squad's machine gunner had been shot right between the eyes. Poor, gentle Smitty; I couldn't believe what I saw. I later learned that as he moved forward under fire to get to a vantage point to open up with the M-60, and as he lifted up his head over a log to see, he was instantly shot. These huge firefights with many weapons firing constantly has a way of really shaking your psyche near oblivion.

Our Cobra gunships came on push, and I was never so glad

to hear anything so beautiful. "Eagle Three Alpha, Eagle Three Alpha, this is Cora Striker, over", called the command pilot. "Cobra Striker this is Eagle Three Alpha", we will pop smoke around our location, but need firing to

"Smitty" Wayne Smith was killed and Sgt. David Stansfield was shot up very badly on Hill 882. Dave Stansfield was the Squad Leader as they walked into an ambush trying to recon the area, and Smitty was the machine gunner

our north about 50 mikes to the front of the smoke, over", responded the RTO for third squad. "Roger, waiting for the smoke, then north, copy?" asked the pilot, "Copy that Striker, out".

"Pop smoke, pop smoke in front of your locations", the RTO yelled as loud as he could. Those farther away from him may not have heard him, but when they saw the others closer to him throwing smoke grenades as far as they could out in front of them, they did the same. In came the Cobra Gunships with the "fewwww, fewww, fewww, fewww", as the rockets were fired, and "boom, boom, boom, boom", as they exploded on top of the enemy positions. The rocket firing was simultaneous to the miniguns that fired four thousand rounds per minute in a "grrrrrrrrrrrrrr, grrrrrrrrrr" noise of the super-fast Gatling-like guns.

While the Cobras were making their runs, we moved quickly as the enemy was being obliterated from above, and got a hold of everyone wounded and dead, and pulled back to a point where artillery could be directed. We called to the Cobra's to inform them that we were calling in artillery so they could get out before the rounds started coming in.

"Fire mission…Fire Mission", called the Lt. to the artillery supporting us, while he looked at his map coordinates. "Fire a marking round, coordinates Charlie two niner, Foxtrot five six, over", went his command. "Roger ", was the response. Marking rounds were white smoke rounds sometimes used to mark a target. Seconds later the round came in. "Red-leg, add five zero mikes and fire HE rounds for effect" Red-leg was a nickname for our artillery guys, and he was telling them to add 50 meters to the first round and fire High Explosive (HE) rounds until told to stop. When the rounds came in, he could adjust them toward the enemy if they weren't right where he wanted them. After killing some and running the rest of the enemy off, we returned to the company and many more battles to come.

This battle was not like others I had been in, and I could feel there was really something different here. The enemy was not retreating out of the area as in times past. They were dug into the mountain and did not plan to move. Also this was the NVA, well trained and determined to fight. They were in large numbers, well equipped, and ready for a showdown. As a result, we had to constantly be on our toes and not let our guard down.

The knowledge that we were constantly being watched, targeted, and living right in the midst of the enemy was not at all comforting. There was no such thing as being on guard while others could relax off duty. We were all on duty twenty-four seven causing our tensions to rise. We were set up in platoon size units, approximately 45 or so men in four squads, and had some distance between those platoons.

The next night about two am, excuse me, 0200 hours, I was on guard at our position along the NDP. Not much had been happening that evening other than the occasional artillery flare over us, where you'd hear the pop of the flare separating from the artillery shell, then the feww, feww, feww noise of the artillery shell falling to the ground from way up high, end over end.

All of a sudden a fierce firefight broke out at third platoon's position, some 100 to 150 yards away from us. We heard the ensuing grenade explosions, RPG and machine guns, and claymore mines exploding. I felt completely helpless and listened in on my radio as the CO was directing a squad or two from another platoon to move to help them. He was warning the RTO of the guys fighting to make sure not to shoot at the reinforcements coming to them from the south.

The next day we heard that a couple of our guys had been killed and about twelve of the enemy. We all knew we had really walked into it this time, and this was certainly the worst battle I had ever been in with no sign of getting better. The CO called into the Gulf of Tonkin to our Navy battleships and had them pound the mountain with their eight inch guns. That hill shook all night and finally morning came. This next day was one I will never forget.

CHAPTER FIFTEEN

BATTLE FOR HILL 882

"Dick, quick, bring that radio to me" yelled the Lieutenant over the noise of AK-47's opening up on them, as they suddenly realized we were surrounded, and being fired at from every side. I was carrying the radio for this patrol and began moving forward when I heard an explosion on top of the ridge line. Lt. Richardson crawled back to the edge of the ridgeline where I was slowly moving forward while firing my rifle. "Mac hurry with the radio" shouted the LT, while blood was running down his face from shrapnel of the grenade that exploded and had hit him. I jumped up to a crouching position and ran with my upper body parallel to the ground, hoping not to get hit. I knew we were in desperate trouble and that the lieutenant wanted to call for artillery support.

Before I got to Lt. Richardson, I was shaken to the ground by another explosion not far from where I stood. I got back up and pushed some jungle ferns out of my way to see Lt. Richardson on the ground with his arm nearly blown off, trying to regain control of his senses. I positioned myself in front of and slightly to the left of the Lieutenants position in an attempt to hold off the attackers until help would arrive. It was then that Lt. Richardson got up and grabbed his arm with his other hand, and tried to move back off of the ridgeline.

"LT, get down, get down", was yelled loudly as Lieutenant Richardson, who was already critically wounded, got up to run out of the burning napalm to thicker cover. Those words were no sooner yelled when his neck was ripped open and blood flying, as a bullet came tearing through it.

"LT", I yelled as he was turned around from the impact to his neck, stumbled and fell. He had already been hit by shrapnel above his left eye, and had a satchel charge land and explode a feathers width away from his arm, which was now hanging by some skin. The crimson mess that used to be his forearm was being held with his other hand. It looked bad, and it was bad and not much chance of survival for this brave Airborne Ranger officer, but we had to try.

Sgt. Tom Brennan and I were the only ones able to still fire and hopefully hold off the enemy till help might arrive. I fired my M-16 until the barrel became white hot and ceased to function. I thought I was finished when I remembered LT's M-16, which he could no longer use. I reached for the weapon and began to fire. Tom and I were just trying to keep alive for a few more minutes, just a little more time and they would break through to us. At least we kept thinking that would happen and hoped it would be soon.

All of a sudden an enemy Chicom grenade landed just a few feet in front of me. I reached for the grenade and threw it back, but it never exploded, thank God. We had obviously been surrounded and fire was coming at us from everywhere. It seemed like a hopeless situation to survive, and I had to fight my mind to keep it focused on fighting and not let myself give in to the death-grip of fear that kept pulsating in my thoughts. We just kept firing and firing at sounds never knowing if we hit them or not, while bullets kept hitting all around us.

The sound of our "16's" and the enemy AK-47's popping filled the air with such mind crushing noise that I thought I would never hear well again. Tom yelled, "Dick, lookout" as an NVA satchel charge landed just out of my reach. I buckled as it exploded, throwing me five feet into the air. As I hit the ground I looked and felt to see if I was blown up or missing any limbs. A few seconds later I reached for LT's weapon and again began firing. Tom said, "You OK?" I mumbled something like "couldn't be better" and for a brief, split second reprieve of the horror that was going on around us, we half smiled then began firing again.

When we walked into this ambush 20 minutes prior, four of us were moving a couple of hundred meters in front of the Company to recon the area. After initial enemy contact earlier in the day, the Company had pulled back to the LZ to Medevac the wounded. There we surrounded the LZ to secure it, and called in napalm strikes to the Navy carriers in the Gulf of Tonkin.

"Eagle One, Eagle One, this is Dragon 6, over," came the call from the F-4 Phantom pilots as they approached our remote spot in the jungle. "Dragon 6, this is Eagle One, we will pop purple smoke for identification, over," said Capt. Faulkenberry in response to the call. "Eagle One I copy purple smoke, over." "Roger" said the Captain.

The CO then yelled to those surrounding the LZ, "Pop Purple Smoke in front of each position". We then heard that familiar sound of pop, pop-pop, pop, pop, followed by the shuashuashuauaas sound of escaping smoke as the smoke grenades pins were pulled and thrown.

"Eagle One, Dragon 6, we acknowledge purple smoke, over". Dragon 6, Eagle One, we need napalm and HE rounds dropped 200 mikes to the west of our smoke, over". Roger Eagle One, copy 200 meters west of your location, copy?" "Copy and Roger Dragon 6", over." "Eagle One we're approaching the target from the east so get your heads down, over". "Dragon 6, Roger that."

As the Phantoms rolled out we could barely see through the trees. We heard the soft roar of the jet engines in the distance as they made their final turn to the target area.

An F-4 Phantom Jet turns for a bombing run in support of the infantry ground troops calling for their help. Close-in support of air power was instrumental in victories of entrenched enemies

As they drew closer to us the soft roar grew louder until it was deafening. I could see brief glimpses of the napalm pods as they dropped from the F-4's wings, and began their end over end roll toward the target area behind us. It looked like the bombs were coming right at us, and we dropped and hugged the ground. I clearly heard the foomp…foomp foomp of the pods as they passed over the tree tops above us, and then the fuuuuuurrrrrhhhhh of the igniting napalm as it hit its target.

The air strike lasted all of ten minutes as the four planes made their runs. "Eagle One this is Dragon 6, we have a significant burning target area and we're heading home, over". Dragon 6, Eagle One, we appreciate the help, over." "Roger Eagle One, glad to do it, call us anytime; Dragon 6 out." As the drone of the jet engines faded away, we wondered how soon we would need them again, and I felt a brief moment of isolation with their absence.

Then came the call, "Eagle Five, Eagle One, over." LT Richardson, our platoon leader was Eagle Five, and we all knew what the CO wanted. "Eagle One, this is Five, over". "Five, I want you to send four men up to recon the air strike, over" "Eagle One, Eagle Five, Roger."

As a few of us stood near to Lt. Richardson, fear broke out on our faces like a rash, hoping not to be chosen. We had been trying to take this hill (mountain) for several days, with numerous casualties. The North Vietnam Army (NVA) had a massive tunnel complex inside this mountain that had been there for years dug deep into the rock, and we knew they would be there waiting in ambush for us. The same scenario had been happening all week. We would have the jets come in during daylight and drop massive bomb loads, and the ships in the Gulf of Tonkin would fire all night with eight inch guns. We would then move up, only to have an entrenched enemy waiting to pick us off.

"Smitty you have point, I'll walk slack, Tom, you're middle, Dick, carry the radio and walk rear guard." I was panic-stricken! You get through a war by not knowing what you're going to get into on any given day, but this was different; this was suicide! We all knew good and well that the enemy was waiting, having been in the safety of the tunnels during the air strike, only to come out in force and lay in ambush. Now a platoon of thirty to forty men wasn't moving ahead to face the inevitable with more numbers, but four of us were moving ahead alone to be cut off and killed. This was nothing but a death trap, and I didn't like the odds.

"I'm not going sir," I said as if I had a choice. LT looked at me with an incredulous stare. "Yes you are", he said. "Saddle Up!" "No sir" I said, trying to stand my ground. The LT looked at me again and said, "We have direct orders from the CO to recon the area; do you want to get court martialed?" I was stunned by the term and I had never refused, nor thought it possible for me to refuse a direct order, and certainly didn't want to be court martialed.

"LT", I said, "You know this is crazy. We're going to be killed up there, and for what?" Smitty chimed in surprising me. "LT, Dick's right. We're going to be sittin' ducks for those gooks up there". Tom, (Sergeant Brennan), even said, "LT, I think they're right, we're going to get killed up there!" Lt. Richardson knew none of us had been cowards, and had always done as ordered before. He said, "Well what do you want me to do?" I said, "Call the CO and tell him we don't want to go because of the last days experiences doing the same thing". "It won't do any good but I'll try", said the Lieutenant.

"Eagle One, Eagle Five, over". "Go ahead Five, over." "Sir, the men don't want to go to recon the area because they said the enemy is waiting for us as in the last few days, over". "Five, you tell the men they need to recon that area. We have hit them all night with Navy guns, and now have napalmed them also. The enemy is dead; get me a body count, over." One, this is Five, roger, out".

We were all standing next to the LT when he called, and knew our fate was sealed. Lieutenant Richardson looked at us and said, "We gotta Go, but let's say a prayer first". The four of us put out hands in the center of the circle we made, as in football huddles, and LT offered up a prayer to protect us. We then headed out.

Two hundred meters in triple canopy jungle might as well have been two miles. We moved out using a cut path, allowing about twenty feet between us. Smitty, who had been a Hell's Angel biker before the war, was walking point. Using hand signals, we stopped and started several times as Smitty would listen and look for movement to our front and sides. As we got to the target area of the napalm strike, it felt extremely eerie. The area in front of us was now open, burned out jungle and still smoldering from the napalm. It was too quiet...too quiet, and I didn't like it. Smitty started over the top of a ridge very slowly. He disappeared from my sight. I whispered loudly, "LT, I don't like it; it'stoo quiet!" I no sooner got those words out of my mouth when the shattering noise of a machine gun broke the silence, and we heard Smitty yell.

We fell to the ground and returned fire. We fired semi-automatic quickly to conserve ammo, but to put out enough base of fire to keep heads down. Smitty had been hit on top of the ridge where we couldn't see him, and the rest of us were lying in the open on smoldering ground trying to decide what to do. Lt. Richardson crawled up and over the top of the ridge, and out of sight. Tom crawled up after him as I began firing all around us. I heard a grenade explosion on top of the ridge. As I looked up, Lt. Richardson had crawled back to call me, and was bleeding from his eyebrow. "Dick, get the radio up here", he yelled. It was then I realized all three were up on top of the ridge, and I was alone on the open, burning side. I started to receive fire from all around me, and realized we had been surrounded.

I began to cry as I waited to be hit by the bullets hitting all around me. I prayed out loud in the noise, "Father, if you get me out of this I'll be your man for good....please Lord...get me out of this". I started to move forward shooting with one hand and reaching for my radio with the other.

The CO had been yelling into his radio from the time the firing had started, but I wasn't about to answer him and let go of my 16 for anything at first. All I could think about was getting to the others and out of this clearing, while putting out as much firing as I possibly could. Finally, as I got to the other side of the clearing, and began crawling into the brush I began to realize the situation looked hopeless.

I grabbed my radio handset and called in desperation, "Eagle One, Eagle One, this is Eagle Five Alpha, we are surrounded and Smitty's been hit, and so has Eagle Five, over". I was yelling into the radio handset and was in a flat panic. The CO's voice came back over the radio, "Now settle down son, and tell me your situation, over". Sir, help us, we're in big trouble, need immediate assistance, over". "Five Alpha, you're going to have to hold out as you are surrounded, and we have been trying to break in your rear door since the firing began, and have met heavy resistance; you copy, over"? "Sir, I don't want to die; you've got to get to us" The CO's voice was becoming urgent. "We'll get there as soon as we can, just hang on, hang on, Alpha, out"

While I was firing, and being terribly perplexed that my magazines of ammo were being used too quickly, I managed to crawl forward. By the time I got to the LT, he was in bad shape. Tom had run down the ridge to our rear to see if he could get reinforcements through, but couldn't. He ran back up under fire next to me. It then dawned on me that there was no sign of Smitty; what happened to Smitty? He was the reason we all went forward; to get him out.

It was then that LT Richardson got up, and was shot. Tom tried to stop his bleeding, and I was firing with everything I had from behind a small tree branch. All of a sudden I heard the familiar blasting noise of an M-60 Machine Gun behind us. I turned my head to see, and running up the ridge with the M-60 under one arm, and a long belt of ammo over the other was Mark Bogio, firing from the hip, and cutting trees down; killing the enemy. I said, "John Wayne you better get down" to which he smiled and said "You guys get outta here". I then saw Dennis Buckingham, Sgt. Ray Neiman, Oliver Jefferson and other men from our platoon coming up the ridge, firing at a retreating enemy, and thanked God we were saved.

I slid down the ridge on my hands, slightly burning them as I went on the smoldering napalm. When I got to the base of the ridge, I saw Smitty lying face down in the brush, with blood spurting out of the top of his head. The top of his scalp had been ripped open by the machine gun fire we first heard. I put a large dressing over the wound and yelled for a Medic.

We started to receive more fire from our left, so I got out in front of Smitty and the Medic, and returned fire until Smitty was ready to be moved. There were about ten of us now, and we attempted to regroup between shooting at the enemy, and the explosions of grenades and RPG's all around us. We knew we had been re-surrounded since the rest of our squad had broken through to us, but we had to get Smitty and LT to the LZ for medevac or they would soon be dead.

Sgt. Ray Nyman took point and started out, while Jeff (Oliver Jefferson) walked his slack. I grabbed Smitty, and put his arm over my shoulder, and got us to our feet. I

Sgt. Ray Nyman　　　　　　Oliver Jefferson

Sgt. Nyman led the squad that broke through to us on Hill 882 when we were pinned down and Lt. Richardson was killed. Oliver Jefferson, who I always called Jeff was one of them that came after us

realized Smitty was in shock from his wound and blood loss, but managed to help him put one foot in front of the other as we moved out. We walked about 30 meters or so when two gooks opened fire on us from the undergrowth not twenty yards from us. The bullets they fired ripped the bark off of a tree we were just getting to. I dropped Smitty to the ground, brought my M-16 up and sprayed the brush they were firing from. Although I couldn't see them, their firing stopped, and I assumed I had sent them to meet Buddha.

I dropped to my knees and began to recheck Smitty, who was trying his best to stay conscious. I heard some movement coming up behind me, and as I turned quickly I saw Doc our Medic and another man carrying the LT on a makeshift stretcher. "He's dead Dick, LT is dead", Doc said as a familiar sad expression came over him. "Oh hell", I said, choking back the feeling of despair. "Well we gotta get Smitty back to the LZ for a Medevac or he's next. Come on, let's move out".

We began to move again when Jeff yelled for us all to get

Depiction of heavy firing going on and just trying to beat back the enemy so getting out of there would be possible

down. "They're commin' up the sides", he said as we found ourselves on a small finger ridge of the mountain. "Move into a perimeter", Sgt. Nyman yelled as I put Smitty down in the middle of the trail. We formed a circle around him and began to saturate the brush around us with intense firepower from our weapons. Some threw grenades between the bursts of gunfire, and we realized the enemy had stopped coming up the finger. "Cease Fire, cease-fire" Sgt. Nyman yelled. "Ok, move out". I grabbed Smitty and started out again.

After what seemed like an eternity, we made contact with the outer LZ guards of our platoon. "Strike Force, Strike Force" they yelled as they heard us coming, which was the code word of our unit. If they didn't hear it back instantaneously, they would fire on us thinking we were the enemy. "Strike Force...Strike Force...Strike Force...Strike Force" was yelled back to them by about four of us to make sure the already trigger nervous trail guards wouldn't fire at us.

We made it, I thought to myself. HALLELUJAH! Even though we were still surrounded by the enemy, we were back to much larger numbers of at least thirty or so. I took Smitty to the edge of the LZ where many wounded lay in waiting for medevac choppers. Tom was walking in half shock with a blank stare on his face, and I realized I was not hearing well from the satchel charge and probably half in shock myself. Doc Minks, the CP medic asked me if I could stay out instead of being medevac'd. "We need every man we've got", he said. I indicated I couldn't hear him well from the explosions near me, and he decided to medevac me with the others.

After a fifteen-minute wait or so, another medevac came for those of us who weren't critical. The medics began to load us quickly as they had received fire coming in to get us. I was the last one to get on the left side of the chopper, and half hanging out of the door. As the chopper began to lift off the ridge of the mountain, the pilots began yelling, "Hold On...Hold On...we're going down". My mind was becoming confused at this point and I couldn't believe we were falling from the sky. I hadn't heard any fire toward our chopper.

What was happening...what was happening...no, no, NO...this can't be....we're going to crash...crash. I remember those words playing over and over as we fell. Fortunately, we didn't fall a great distance, and the pilots managed to manipulate the impact to a livable jar. However we had fallen onto another finger ridge of the one we were on and the chopper was leaning and perched on one skid. The blade of the chopper was nearly scraping the ground, and I felt like I was in a dream in slow motion. The blade seemed to be closer and closer to hitting the ground, and the noise it made of the whop...whop... whop...whop...whop seemed to stand out as a warning of eminent disaster. The pilot screamed, "get these men off fast; I can't hold it much longer". Without hearing much of what he said, I could tell what I needed to do. I jumped out of the door and began to pull guys out, hoping we were not going to be cut in two by the chopper's blade.

As we got more men off the medevac, the pilot was able to use the weight shift to upright the chopper from its leaning stance, and avoid the danger of the blade hitting the ground. Later someone told me that the pilot had said that we had loaded too much weight by putting too many wounded on the chopper. There were several of us who were ambulatory, and we reloaded about half the wounded. The pilot then was able to lift straight up and land on the original LZ we had taken off from. I carried a wounded guy over my shoulder, and climbed back up to the LZ. Some of the men on the LZ came down to the rest of the wounded and carried them back up to the top of the ridge.

About twenty minutes later, another Medevac chopper came in for those of us who were left. We flew to Camp Eagle and landed next to the tent hospital. As I got off the chopper, a large artillery piece went off right over my head, and I fell in the mud, only to wake up later on a stretcher in the hospital. I evidently had been holding back all of the fear and exhaustion I had been feeling, but it was now wearing me down and actually making me feel weak. The artillery shot was the last straw to just cause me to fall and pass out.

"Dick...Dick, wake up, wake up". I looked up and saw

Tom Brennan shaking me out of my daydreams and back to reality. "They're releasing us and we gotta get back to the company area and report in; you ok?" Tom asked. "Yeah, I guess; how long have we been here, any way", I asked. "Several hours", he said, "You've been conked most of that time" "I can hear a little better, I said, "but I feel like I'm in a Daze". "Probably the concussion you got from that satchel charge", Tom replied. We left the hospital and began the 3/4 mile walk down the main road in our base camp to our company area.

"Dick, you know when we get back to the company area, Top is going to want to send us right back out to the hill, don't ya", Tom said with a bit of consternation. "Yeah, but we haven't been released for the field yet, and probably won't be for a couple of days, and I'm going on R&R in a couple of days, so it's so long Nam and Hello Taiwan", I said with great relief after just glancing at my Seiko watch and realizing the date.

We arrived in the company area, and reported to the First Sergeant. "You guys released for field duty?" he asked the minute we walked into the hooch. "Not yet and Top, I go on R&R day after tomorrow, so not for at least another week", I said smugly. "What about you Sgt. Brennan?" he asked Tom. "You OK to go back out?" "No", Tom replied, "I have to report for treatment every day for the next week to keep infection out of these wounds". "Ok, you lob cocks stow your gear in an empty hooch out back, and I'll deal with you later".

The couple of days I helped out in the orderly room, where I learned to do the morning report and work with the AR's (Army Regulations) books. Tom was also assigned duty in the company area until his release would come sometime later. The horrific battle carried on with more battalions going in, and I sure hoped that the mess would be over before I got back from R&R.

CHAPTER SIXTEEN

A BREAK FROM THE FIGHT – R & R

The day that I departed for Taiwan, it felt good to be cleaned up and have on a dress uniform for the trip. I met one of the guys from another platoon named Medina, who was also going to Taiwan. He was from Puerto Rico and never let me forget it, as he loved his home and talked about it all of the time.

The unbelievable difference from departing deadly combat and death everywhere, to a place of a big city with the regular life going on of so many was quite mind-boggling. Here in Taiwan there was absolutely no clear understanding of what was going on 1,000 miles from them in Vietnam.

After talking to some soldiers at the airport who were leaving, Medina and I caught a cab from the airport to the Orient Hotel, which was a large luxurious American owned hotel. The cab drivers in Taiwan nearly scared us to death speeding, and what I thought was recklessly driving through heavy traffic in the city. It struck me funny that here we were, brave warriors from a war holding on to our seats with "white-knuckles" as these drivers negotiated the traffic. "Hey man, slow down" we yelled to deaf ears as the cab driver just nodded and smiled and kept up his pace.

We checked in to the hotel and changed quickly to the "civvies" we had with us. We then went down and had a big steak dinner with all of the trimmings, and just relished in the food, comfort, and quiet of a normal life.

The next day we took a tour of the island and just were in awe of the beauty surrounding us. The way they layered rice paddies from the sides of mountains was a lovely sight, which made great use out of all of the land for rice production.

Tiered mountainsides allowed the farmers to make use of ordinarily unusable terrain to grow rice.

Coming back from the island tour, we went into a tailor shop and I was fitted for two suits. We bought some other clothes and it just felt great to be out of uniform and go and do whatever we wanted.

The third day we started to walk up the circular driveway of a beautiful building that we thought must be a museum. Unfortunately, it was the President's palace, and we were quickly confronted by armed guards demanding we turn around and go back. They of course spoke in Chinese, and we had no idea what they were saying, but we certainly understood the guns pointing at us and were not about to argue.

We ended up going to see a movie which was just released called Butch Cassidy and the Sundance Kid. It seemed strange to see an American movie spoken in Chinese with English translations written at the bottom of the screen. The week we were there was peaceful and a greatly needed break from the horrors of war.

Preparing to return to Vietnam with five more months in combat created a tense and unsettling feeling that grew as we approached the country. We flew into Da Nang coming back from Taiwan, and Medina and I went different directions. I ran into another trooper from my unit near the air base and recognized him but wasn't sure of his name. He came up to me and said "You're McBain?" "Yeah, you're Jones...third platoon aren't you?" I asked in return. "Yeah" he replied. "You know we're still trying to take that hill", he said. "We lost the biggest part of the battalion, well mostly wounded, but beaucoup killed also. As a matter of fact, the second platoon...you're in the second platoon aren't you?" he asked almost too cautiously to suit me. "Yeah, Why?" I said. "Man I'm sorry, I was told that counting you there are only three of you left for duty".

I couldn't believe my ears! What about all of my buddies? "What happened?" I said in dismay. "Overrun at night, but most of the guys are not dead though; as a matter of fact, most are out there on that hospital ship", he said while directing my attention to the large white ship with a red cross in the bay. "They're out there"? I asked urgently. "Yeah, most were transported here yesterday and going home with million dollar wounds", he claimed shaking his head. "I'll see you later", I said while starting away.

I muttered to myself, "I've got to get out to that ship". Jones yelled back at me as I was heading toward the dock area, "Hey McBain, you're getting the Bronze Star "V", he said. I stopped in amazement. "What for?" I yelled back.

"For that Hill", he said. I paid little attention to his reply because I had already started back running toward the docks. As I drew closer to the dock that had the launch to take people out to the hospital ship, I saw a launch half way out to the ship. I went up to one of the Navy guys and said, "I have to get out to that ship; my buddies are out there".

Hospital Ship in Da Nang Harbor where all of my buddies had just been evacuated to. I missed the last launch so I waved down a chopper lifting off and although the pilot was furious, a Major told him to take me out to the ship. I got to see them before they went home

"Sorry Mac, that's the last launch going out today", he replied. I walked away feeling such a sense of loss, especially being so close to where my friends were and not being able to see them again before they went home.

As I was mulling over what I could do to get out to that ship, I heard a chopper begin to rev its engines to my left. I looked up and saw a "slick" getting ready to lift off with several officers in it. I ran as fast as I could to the helo-pad waving my arms, and shouting,"Hey...Hey...Hey..." The chopper had lifted straight up, and was about fifteen feet in the air when the pilot saw me, and brought the chopper back down on the pad.

"What is it", he shouted over the chopping sound of the

blade. "I need to get out to that hospital ship", I yelled back at him. A furious look came over his face and he yelled, "Get your butt off of this pad, we're taking off". As he started to rev his engines for lift off, a Major in the rear seat motioned me to come closer. "What do you need", he yelled. "Most of my buddies are on that hospital ship, and I have to see them, and the last boat has already left", I yelled at the top of my lungs. The Major tapped the pilot on his shoulder, and said, "Let's take him out there". The pilot looked at the Major in an annoyed fashion, then turned to me and resentfully said, "Get on".

We flew out to the ship and the pilot landed the chopper on the medevac pad on deck. I jumped off and turned to both the Major and the pilot and yelled, "Thanks a lot man, I appreciate it". They both gave me a thumbs-up and took off. It was then it dawned on me that what I did was pretty bold and may have caused me some trouble. I was thankful the Major in the seat had been a good guy and had me brought out there.

I found the first sailor I could and got directions to a nurse's station, where I was directed to a large ward that contained most of my friends. "Hey, McBain", how'd you get here?" they asked. I was busy sizing up their wounds. Some looked real bad, and had blood all over their bandages, while others looked real depressed but seemed to lighten up when they saw me.

"What are you lob cocks doing...always looking for ghost time?" I said as I squeezed through the narrow lanes between their bunks. Ghost-time was unscheduled time out of the jungle due to some malady like dysentery, malaria, jungle-rot, and the like. Although it was for something you didn't want, it was time out of combat and so was thought of positively.

All of a sudden the room became quiet and serious looks were on all of their faces. "Mac, don't go back...they'll send you right back to the hill...it's a massacre out there". "Tell me what happened", I said. Sgt. Bishop who had been my first squad leader related when most of them got hit. "Man, we were set up as always for night and sometime late or early the next day we were overrun. We couldn't tell who was the enemy and who were our guys and the gooks were everywhere; everyone was firing wildly just trying to stay alive", he related.

"It started with an enemy grenade thrown right between Billy and Mike who were asleep; they never knew what hit them", he continued. "I kept crawling toward our guy's positions saying, it's me, brother Bishop, don't shoot. I never saw anything like it! Everyone was shooting everywhere and it was total chaos", he concluded. Some of my other buddies chimed in agreement with Bishop's assessment, and I could see the atmosphere was getting bad, and some were even tearing-up as they remembered that night, and being over-run.

Just then a loudspeaker announcement was made that the last launch was leaving in five minutes. It was then quick good-byes as we fought back feelings knowing we would probably never see each other again. "You lob cocks take care, and give my love to the world when you get there", I said as I walked out of the bay area they were in and back to oblivion, and now, without most of those I had gone through it with to this point.

On the trip back to Camp Eagle I was having a troubling, internal fight with myself. If they are still out there fighting for that worthless hill, am I going to be willing to give my life for it? Then I would think that the guys need everyone they can get out there, and how could I not go out to help them. I then thought about how most of my guys aren't out there anymore and it would be a whole new mess. I then thought that it was the 101st fighting out there, no matter who is left and it's my duty to go. I hoped against hope that the battle had come to an end.

I was put on a C-130 for the trip back to Phu Bai AFB, and then trucked over to Camp Eagle. I was now even more scared about going back out on that hill after hearing the account of my buddies. I jumped out of the truck, and just stared at our company orderly room feeling numb. I was trying to decide what I was going to do, because unbelievably there was a choice, although not a good one. I slowly walked into the orderly room.

CHAPTER SEVENTEEN

HUGE MISTAKE – ALMOST

"Hi Top, I'm back", I said as I walked into the company orderly room. "And none too soon...Get your weapon, C-Rations, and Ammo, and report to the chopper pad ASAP. We need you bad out there...gettin' our butts kicked", said Sgt. Manning, who had been out there with us until he took over as Company First Sergeant. "Top I saw our guys on the hospital ship in Da Nang on my way back. They had quite a horrific story to tell. Any chance you might need some help here for a few days? I asked. "Not a chance...we need every able bodied man out there and quickly", was his response. "Now get your gear!"

After taking a deep breath and feeling like a coward, I couldn't believe what was coming out of my mouth. "Top, I'm not going back out there", I said as forcefully and clearly as I could. "Yes you are, and you better get moving now", he angrily replied. "Top, I'm going to Re-up and get out of here now! That's suicide for nothing and a hill that will just go back to the enemy once we take it, and I'm not giving my life for that hill" I said heatedly with my voice raised.

Sgt. Manning was my superior, but also my friend since we fought together in the jungle. "He calmed down and said, "Dick, you know it's your prerogative to re-up any time you want. If that's what you want to do, I'll call Battalion and have the papers drawn up, and you'll be on your way home tomorrow" Top said. Well re-upping was not at all what I wanted to do. It meant three more years in the Army, and probably another full year here in combat. On the other hand, it was an immediate ticket home for a 30-day leave, and, especially, away from that hill.

Top made the call to battalion to get the paper work started. "Get your weapon ready for turn-in, and check with S-4 for your uniforms and personal belongings, then check back with me", he said. "Top, I...." "Don't worry about it", he quietly said. He knew I was not a coward, but a college kid who got drafted, and sent to a war I didn't believe in, but was trying to do my patriotic duty. I turned away and walked outside feeling very wrong and cowardly.

My mind was unclear; a confusing jumble of thoughts. I knew they needed me, and many more men out on that hill, but I didn't want to die on it. It meant three more years in the Army, and at least one of them here in Vietnam, but home in a couple of days. What am I going to do? I don't know but just get outta here...that's all...to safety of the World; but what about those guys out there? What should I do? I spent the next hour agonizing over these thoughts. As I got to battalion headquarters, the clerks there had all my papers ready to be signed. I started to read them, but couldn't concentrate. What should I do? What should I do?

I looked up at the clerks who were standing over me like vultures waiting to grasp the papers out of my hand as soon as I signed them. They must have gotten a bonus or something for getting guys to re-up. They of course were oblivious to the mental torment going on within me, and there was no one to talk to, or counsel me about the right or wrong in making this decision.

I finally realized I would have trouble the rest of my life if I didn't go out and help my brothers in this life or death

struggle. I also came to the realization that it was my duty as a soldier, whether I could get out of it legally or not.
"Sorry guys, I can't do it! I just can't do three more years in this green machine", I announced to them. They looked very angry. "We just typed all this up, and now you're not gonna sign them?" they asked in loud voices. "That's a Roge", I said as I got up to head back to my company area, and a First Sergeant who I knew was going to be angry beyond belief.

Top was waiting for me as I came into the area. They had called him, and he was livid. "Mac, you get your weapon, your C's, and your ammo, along with your dumb butt up to that chopper pad ASAP or I'm gonna shoot you myself", he ranted. "On my way, Top", I said non-chalantly, knowing I wasn't about to get any more sympathy from him.

Stairs (left) to the chopper pad at Camp Eagle. It was a long walk up when I thought I was going back out to Hill 882

I climbed the one hundred or so stairs up to the chopper pad with a full ruck sack, ammo, water, C's, and my M-16. I was expecting a chopper anytime to take me back out to possibly my death. I was afraid, but felt much better since I had made my decision, and at least my mind was now clear.

I waited and waited in the hot sun and kept looking at my watch and wondering where the chopper was. After about half an hour, I was looking out over the terrain and noticed something that looked out of place. Across the sky, probably five or six miles out on the horizon were many black spots. I watched in wonder as they slowly got bigger. Soon it was plain to see they were choppers, forty or fifty of them coming my way. As they began to line up in double file to land on our double pad, I moved to the side and out of the way.

The first birds came in and I saw my company commander, his radio operator and Doc Minks. As Doc jumped off the chopper he said to me, "We finally took that hill! Two

Choppers lining up bringing in what was left of the Battalion after they took Hill 882. Our birds coming in was one of the most joyful times I had in the Nam, and to think I had almost committed to four more years to avoid going where I now would not have to go was very sobering

weeks and much of the battalion as casualties, but we finally took that hill". He was smiling largely as were the others getting off those birds, but one was smiling more than any other; me! I had minutes earlier almost condemned myself to three more years in the military just to avoid going back out to that hill, where I wouldn't have had to go anyway. Thank you Jesus!

It turns out that the hill was finally taken after two weeks of fighting. I was told that the "Recon Platoon", led by Lt. Hill had slack-jumped into the top of the hill, catching the enemy in the middle and taking away their escape route.

In our Battalion area we held a memorial service for our Battalion dead troopers from Hill 882, and it was very emotional. Dear friends were killed, and nearly whole platoons were wounded. Taps and the command to present arms seemed surreal to a guy who just a year earlier was a college student

We held a memorial service for all of the guys who were killed on that hill. It was solemn and sad, yet provided a place to honor these brave men that gave everything for a country that had called them. It was quite moving to see the rifles and boots of our fallen all together, and reminded us of our mortality.

After honoring our dead, they had an awards ceremony for citations given for action on Hill 882. I was given the Bronze Star "V" and a Purple Heart. I was proud but knew I had done no more than many of the other guys on that hill. I think most of the guys who got medals that day felt the same way about those who didn't. I avoided the news people there who wanted stories for the home town papers, but later found out that they got the stories anyway from the Army PR folks. I first discovered that the newspapers

Lt. Col. Shay pinning the Bronze Star "V" on Dick for actions on Hill 882. I was proud but felt awkward because I felt everyone deserved this honor who fought on that hill

had the stories when I called home from a MARS phone the next time I was in the rear. I had never called home from Vietnam but was talked into it when there opened up some free time on the MARS phone while I was in the area.

My mother answered and I said, "Hi Mom, its Dick". My Dad quickly got on another extension and they both sounded concerned." Are you OK?" they both asked almost simultaneously. "I'm fine, how are you?" I responded. "Well we heard that you were wounded and we were wondering…" my mother started to say. "Whoa, Whoa, I'm fine…where did you hear that?" I asked. "The newspaper people called and told us", she said, "and you've been telling us you haven't seen hardly any action and this was a shock".

"Mom, believe me I'm fine, and those people should not have worried you, I'm sorry they did", I replied. "Anyway, I just called to say hi as I was given a minute or two on this MARS phone, and they are telling me that I have to get off", I said. "Oh, well all right, you make sure you write us and tell us all about it", Mom responded. "I will but I got to go…I love you all and will see you soon; bye". The MARS line went dead right then but I sure was glad that I had the chance to speak to my folks.

During the time of rebuilding, Top had me help out in the orderly room. There were many letters to write to parents that we typed up for the CO to send, as well as many citations that were being requested for bravery during that horrendous battle. It was a sad duty as I was brought into the numbers of our guys who were killed while typing letters to their folks. So many were draftees like me who came reluctantly to do their duty, and not because they were career soldiers and this was just the risks of their

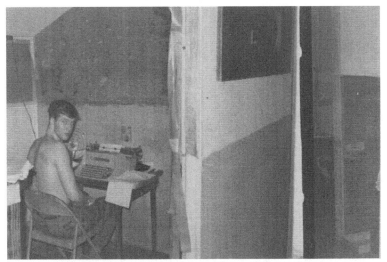
Dick helping out in the Orderly Room at Camp Eagle

careers.

The time in the orderly room would also prove to be very helpful back in the States, although I didn't realize it at the time. Honing my skills at doing the morning reports and the AR's that I had first learned just before leaving for R&R, would open the door for much better duty after I got back from Vietnam.

CHAPTER EIGHTEEN

REPLACEMENTS

SGT. Tom Brennan and Diep with two replacements, Jaco & Don Cordle. Vietnam like all wars was fought by young men, even boys. Jaco and Don here look like kids but were good fighting men, and always carried the fight to the enemy

We were ordered to stand-down to rebuild our units in receiving new reinforcements and training them in our SOP's. Some of the guys coming in looked like young kids, but the truth was that most of us were all kids fighting a war ten thousand miles from home.

After the taking of Hill 882, three of us with experience were each made squad leaders, and took on mostly a whole new squad of soldiers just in from training in the states. The replacements seemed eager and now we were the guys everyone looked to for direction and knowhow.

It struck me quite strange that seven and a half months earlier I was the new guy depending on, and looking for answers from the leaders who were in charge at the time. How quickly it seemed for me to go from "Cherry" to the leader, and in charge of the most critical of life and death decisions at times. Anyway, that's the way it went and when it's your time you have to step up to the plate.

Once we had all of our guys together for my squad, we had a meeting where I explained our SOP (Standard Operational Procedures) to insure that they had a beginning idea of how we operate. There were a lot of questions, especially from those who were concerned of what we might be facing, and I tried to allay their fears with positive replies. I was glad to have the chance to point out things most of us had to learn as we went.

"First", I said, "We watch out for each other and work as a team. Everyone will do his part and carry his own weight. We're in the midst of the hot season, so I want you to carry plenty of water. You guys who don't are not to come crying when you run out and want someone else to give you what they had the good sense to carry when you wouldn't. These ruck sacks are heavy already but I carry eleven quarts of water during the hot season."

"You need to go to supply and get more canteens. They issued you two one quarts. Tell them you need two of the two quarts, and a five quart blivit-bag. These five-quarts also serve as a nice pillow at night."

"Everyone in the squad needs at least two bandoleers of magazines for their M-16, and you can carry more in your rucksack if you like because you don't want to run out of ammo when the shit hits the fan. Also, everyone is to carry a hundred rounds of machine gun ammo in or on top of their rucks, and one claymore making sure it has a firing device with it. Have at least one trip flare if not two with you, and several of you will be carrying a LAW on the side of your rucks."

"Speaking of Rucks, we use the kind that has the quick releases when we make contact. For me, it's better to fall to the ground and then release them, as they stick sometimes and you don't want to be standing fighting your shoulder straps while Charlie is trying to drill you."

"We carry a four day resupply of food in the rucks, which is basically a case of C's, so make sure you keep enough and don't throw away the stuff you don't like and then complain you've run out of food. Trade cans you don't like with someone who wants to trade what they don't like."

"Usually a new guy gets the radio because its twenty-five pounds plus a couple of batteries. I'll let you know if I want someone to carry the radio for me, but for now I'm used to it, and have just been in the habit of having that communication with me at all times."

"Now the other new guy prize", I continued, "is the M-60 machine gun, again usually because of its weight. Old timers feel they have paid the price already and usually pass it down to the new guy. Since we have ten new guys I will first ask if someone wants to carry the gun before arbitrarily assigning it. Ok; anyone?" "Specialist, I'll carry it", was the response from one of the smallest men. "What's your name again trooper?" I asked as I couldn't recall. "I'm called shorty by the guys who know me", he said. "Shorty, I have other things in mind for you, so if you don't mind, I'll get someone else, but thanks for volunteering", I said.

"What's your name", I said as I pointed to one of the bigger guys in the group. "Terry Blake", came his response. "Terry how'd you do on the range with the M-60", I asked. "I got the second gun bar', he answered. "OK, you've got the gun for now, so make sure you and…" I looked around and pointed at another of the men, "you, what's your name", I asked him" "Jack Carter", he said. 'You're Terry's Assistant Gunner for now, copy"? I asked. "Roger" he said.

"OK, who wants to carry the thumper" I asked. A man named Melvin raised his hand and said, "I will". "OK" I said. "After our meeting Terry and Mel will come with me to S-4 so they can issue you guys your weapon, or at least sign you up for it as you of course won't get it until we are ready to move out. We also want to make sure that they take you off the list for your 16's so you're not charged for them later".

A day or so later we got orders to go out on an operation, and I made sure all of the guys got the weapons and ammo we needed for the mission. We had checked their rucksacks a day earlier to make sure they had everything they would need or I sent them to S-4 to get it. On top of all of the other stuff, they needed to have a poncho, poncho liner, LSA rifle lubricant and cleaning tools, Bug Juice (Army Bug Repellant), and plastic rifle caps for the M-16's. Since it was the hot season they wouldn't need to hump what we called jungle sweaters, which were in high demand during the monsoon season. After double checking their stuff, and making sure that they had what they needed, I announced, "We are ready to go".

All the squad was now excited because they had been given the go ahead by their squad leader who knew what had to be done to be ready. The guys began to speculate about how they would perform once in combat, and some had the fear that they might "chicken out". When I heard those things I was quick to say that no matter what your level of experience, you'd be a fool if you were not afraid of combat. Then I would reassure them that once it happens, their training would kick in and they would be amazed at what they would do.

I always tried to alleviate the tensions of new guys, just as Bill Nelson and Steve Clement had done for me when I was a "Cherry".

CHAPTER NINETEEN

COMBAT SQUAD LEADER

Dick was a Squad Leader that almost always carried his own radio. Despite the 25 extra pounds of weight to carry, and was almost always passed on to the next "Cherry", he had made the decision early not to be anything but an arms-length from communication

One of the things that griped me was my rank. I had been promoted twice in basic training, and was promoted to Specialist Four (E-4) shortly after coming to the 101st Airborne. One of my two goals when I got to the company was to become an E-5 sergeant. I was put in several times for that rank but never got it. Now I was an acting E-6 Staff

Sergeant, which was supposed to be the rank of a Squad Leader. To become a non-com you had to go before the promotion board. Every time I was put in for an open allocation to E-5 we were in a hot AO or socked-in so bad with clouds that choppers would not take the risk to come out to get us for the meetings of the Promotion Board. To add insult to injury, they did not hold those allocations until they could get us, but gave them to the REMF's (Rear Echelon Mother F_____) instead. I have to explain that we did not have any disdain for the guys in the rear, but only used that term in frustration when they received preference over us; or if they stole our war trophies which happened too many times because we had to send them in to be kept for us.

Now by the terrible loss of men on Hill 882, I was a squad leader which had almost a whole new squad of soldiers just in from training in the states. As the company went out on the next operation, it was the first time in the jungle for all of these new soldiers. Training these fresh replacements was critical; not only to establish their expectations, but to prepare them for what was ahead of them.

I again explained that they had some small choices they could make for themselves such as how much water they wanted to carry, but warned them in the hot season water could be hard to find and if they ran out they shouldn't expect those carrying more to give them what they had to hump for themselves.

I next instructed them about the expenditure of ammo in a firefight. The magazines for our M-16's were twenty-round clips that we loaded with eighteen rounds so as not to hurt the springs in them. Eighteen rounds in a clip did not last long in a firefight. When first making contact we would fire on "Rock and Roll" (Automatic) as we were falling to the ground to put out a heavy base of fire, but then we fired semi-automatic to conserve ammo and have a better aim.

On automatic, eighteen rounds would be gone on the count of two seconds. With semi-automatic, we controlled the speed of fire. I told them some of the guys were always looking for banana clips that held up to thirty rounds. They were hard to find, but some of the guys got some. Others would tape two magazines together to be able to eject one and flip it over for another. "The problem with this", I said, "is many times the clip taped to the one in the gun had its open end facing the ground, and if you dropped in contact, dirt and dust would easily get in and possibly jam the weapon". I warned them that a jammed rifle in a firefight could cost them their lives. I told them I was content to have my bandoleers filled with full magazines and could replace a spent magazine in seconds, and suggested they do the same.

We made a CA into our new AO, and just like it was for me earlier, this was their first helicopter combat assault and some if not all were nervous. I had to remind some of them to get their weapons safety on, and to make sure they held their rifles with the muzzle pointing down so as not to shoot the chopper blade.

We landed and moved out first as a company, and then broke up into platoon size units, and headed for our NDP objectives to set up and get organized. I knew one of us squad leaders was going to be called soon to patrol the way the company was going to be moving, and in the meantime I had the men set up their positions and clean their rifles. It wasn't long when the call came.

"Razor Two, Razor Two, this is Razor's Edge Alpha, over". The assistant radio operator I had selected to monitor the horn told me that the CP was calling me, and handed me the handset. "Razor Edge Alpha, Razor Two, over", I responded using my new call sign. "Razor Two, Razor's Edge wants to meet with you at the CP in five mikes, over". "Roger that Razor's Edge Alpha, Razor Two out".

The command post was about 50 meters away. Before going I told the men to keep their eyes open, stay down, and keep spread out, and to keep all talking low. As I walked down the trail for the briefing I arrived at the CP in a couple of minutes. I sat down with the other Squad and Platoon Leaders, and the CO began.

"OK, Mac", the CO said to me, "I want you to take your squad down this trail east, and recon the area for about one click prior to us moving the same way", he said as he pointed where he wanted us to go on the map. An important detail he filled in was,"before we go the same way". He must have known that some of the leaders didn't go too far out if they were being sent in a direction other than the way the company or platoon was moving.

"You think your guys are ready", he asked, knowing this was their first patrol? "Ready or not, there always has to be a first time", I replied with a forced smile on my face. "Be careful", the CO said, "We suspect enemy patrols in this area". "Roger, Sir", I said, hoping we wouldn't see any.

I got back to my squad, and began to instruct them in what we were going to do, and what to take. "Shorty" had volunteered to walk point, and I had worked with the other guys in the rear, and assigned the machine gun and thumper to the guys with the best firing skills.

"OK, troops, we're going to move down that trail, slowly and carefully. I want everyone watching and listening for VC. Make sure you have a six to ten foot interval between you, and I don't want any clustering to give the enemy a chance to kill two with one shot; clear? ", I said. "Clear" came the response from all nine men who seemed anxious to venture into their first patrol.

"OK, listen up, leave your ruck's here and take two bandoleers of magazines. Gunner take two hundred rounds for the M-60 and Assistant Gunner take another hundred rounds around your neck, along with your two bandoleers for your 16. Take one canteen of water on your pistol belt and leave any jewelry or other clanging crap here. I want no noise and we will use hand signals as we move. Watch my directions if we make contact", I said. "Shorty, you've got point, and I want it slow and easy, but keep your eyes open for booby traps. Mike, you have Smitty's slack so make sure you watch all around him while he's looking for traps, savvy?" I asked. "That's a Roge", he replied.

"I'm going to walk third, and John you walk behind me with the radio. Terry your fifth with the machine gun, Jack sixth as Assistant Gun, Mel seventh with your thumper, Harry you're eighth, Jim ninth, and Tim you're rear guard, so make sure you keep your eyes open behind us, Roger"?, I said. "Roger", they replied.

"If we make contact hit the ground and fire the first magazine on automatic, but watching where you are in relation to the other guys in front of you. We don't want any friendly fire mistakes. Then go to semi-auto to conserve ammo and have better aim," I said.

"Everybody ready", I said, not waiting for a reply, "Let's

get it on". "Smitty, move out" I commanded, and off we went. "Lock and load, and put it on safety", I said as we began to move. We hadn't moved more than one hundred meters down the trail, when I turned around to check on the men behind me. They were all bunched up together, and I shouted in a loud whisper, "Spread out you guys and get at a six foot interval now!"

As I turned back toward our front, I was about three quarters of the way turned around, when I saw Shorty lift his weapon and attempt to fire. His weapon misfired, and the next thing I heard were enemy AK-47's opening up. I saw Shorty going down, and thought he was hit. I did a half back flip to get behind a tree nearby, and saw Mike, Shorty's slack-man running up the trail, and firing his M-16 above his shoulders, then he went down.

The adrenaline hit fast, and I started yelling behind me, "Get the machine gun up here...move up here on line and everybody fire...Mel watch the trees when you fire that thumper". I saw Terry and Jack running up the middle of the trail with the machine gun to get into position. "Get down", I yelled at them, and they immediately fell to the ground. I watched them as I was firing in the direction of the enemy fire. They were fumbling with the belts of ammo for the machine gun, and were having trouble getting it to fire.

I crawled over to them, and pushed Terry out of the way, as I grabbed the belts of ammo, and reloaded the gun. I began firing the M-60 in the direction of the initial firing, then stopped. "OK, keep up the firing...about twenty round bursts...Jack add on your belt of ammo to the end of this belt", I yelled over the deafening noise of gunfire and grenade explosions. "And don't shoot Shorty and Mike; there're over there", I said as I pointed to the left.

I thought Shorty had been hit, and wasn't sure whether Mike dropped down on his own or was hit also. I began to crawl to the left front to see if I could see them. As I moved forward I suddenly realized that I didn't hear any more enemy weapons firing. "Cease fire...cease fire....cease fire", I yelled to my men while motioning with the appropriate hand signal. Seconds later all was quite again. I crawled forward and saw Shorty on his stomach fighting with his M-16, and Mike lying nearby.

"Shorty...Mike...you guys hit", I asked? "No, this damn gun jammed on me", Shorty said. "I'm OK", Mike replied. "OK, everyone just listen for a minute for movement", I said. We couldn't hear anything and I was sure the enemy had di di mau'd. "Keep your eyes fixed in that direction", I said as I pointed in the direction the enemy had run. "We don't know if they're coming back so stay alert", I ordered. "John, get that radio over here", I yelled to my RTO. John crawled over to me quickly, and said, "The CO's been calling for you since the firing began". "OK, give me the horn", I said.

"Razor's Edge, Razor's Edge, Razor Two, over", I called to the CO. "Razor Two this is Razor's Edge, what is happening out there, over", came the CO's reply. "Sir, I'm not sure yet whether we walked into an ambush, or just ran into the enemy, and I'm trying to find out now, over", I replied. "All right Two, anybody hurt, over?" "No casualties Sir and I haven't been far enough out front to see if there are any enemy dead or blood trails yet, over", I explained. "I'm sending Razor's Echo (the field exec) out to you with a medic in case, you copy over?" "Copy, Sir,

I'll get back to you with a sitrep ASAP", I said. "Roger Razor Two, out". It was then that Razor's Echo, a 1st Lieutenant named Hill who was an Airborne Ranger, came running up the trail to our location. "C'mon Mac, let's go get 'em", he said in his usual gung ho demeanor, and proceeded right past me running down the trail, heaving a grenade to the right and then the left as he went. "You guys stay here and be alert", I said to my squad.

I ran after the Lieutenant to make sure he had cover, but fortunately, the enemy was long gone. After going out by ourselves much too far in my opinion, I yelled "LT, they're gone". I was becoming worried that the two of us having ventured out too far by ourselves might just run into the enemy without the help we would need. "OK, let's head back", he said to my relief. LT Hill was a real combat leader, but a little more gung-ho than I liked. He was the one who took his Recon Platoon and slack-jumped into the top of Hill 882, which brought that horrific battle to an end. I was happy he agreed with me to head back, but he'd have been just as happy to continue on in hopes of catching them.

When we got back to the squad, we began asking questions of Shorty and Mike to find out what had happened. It turns out that as Shorty began around a bend in the trail, he came upon a VC patrol moving toward us. The enemy point man was down in a squatting position looking at the trail for tracks. As Shorty came in sight of him, he raised his rifle and fired, but nothing happened. He later discovered his weapon jammed when he went to lock and load as we first began to move out. When his weapon misfired, the enemy point man brought his weapon up to shoot Shorty, and as he fired, Shorty had already begun a quick fall to the ground.

That's when I had looked up and saw him go down as I first heard the enemy fire. Fortunately, he was not hit.

Next Mike, who was walking Shorty's slack, began running forward firing from above his shoulders. Those two small trees that formed an arch in the trail where the enemy point man was squatting, Mike had hit all around the enemy as evidenced by bullet holes in the tree arch, but evidently did not hit the enemy, as we saw no blood anywhere in the area.

As we had moved forward on-line to fire back, the enemy patrol ran away from us. By all appearances, no one on either side was hit with all of the firing going on, and I felt fortunate none of my guys had been wounded or killed. We later laughed about my first patrol as squad leader being one of enemy contact, but no casualties, and a comedy of errors. The CO was upset with me because we didn't get him an enemy body count, but I was glad no one was hurt.

We headed back to our position with the platoon and set up for the night. The stories were flying from these excited guys who had just experienced their first patrol and a firefight. As soldiers do, they were making outrageous claims, and teasing Shorty about his misfire face to face with the enemy. Shorty looked like he was taking it hard, and I chimed in telling him he did just fine, and that all of the guys would have their time of weapons jamming.

I felt it necessary to give the squad a critique on our first contact in order to let them know what was done right and wrong. When we arrived back at the company's position I gathered them together to explain our first contact.
"Ok guys, for the benefit of the next contact we hit we're going to discuss what happened today to learn better ways

for the things that we did wrong", I began. "I want to begin with what you all did right first", I continued. "

"When the firing began I was pleased to see most of you move up on line for effective enemy repelling. You listened when I told you earlier to fire your first magazine on automatic, which as you could see and hear, made it sound like there were more of us than we actually had; it could be the reason the enemy di di mau'd quickly instead of choosing to fight", I explained. "You reloaded quickly and kept a good base of fire moving in the direction of the enemy without hitting any of our own guys, two of which were in that direction. That was very well done", I commented.

"Now there were a number of things we have to improve on right away, and all they will mean is that you have to think and use your common sense to accomplish them", I continued. "Smitty when you walk point your weapon being able to fire can mean whether you live or die, as you almost saw today", I said. Smitty got defensive saying, "Yes but Dick I thought my weapon was ready", he quickly said. "Smitty I am not picking on you so relax. You're the point man and at all times you have to be sure, not think, that your weapon is ready. You may see me from time to time pull my handle back to make sure all is clear in my chamber, and that there is a bullet in it", I told him. Anyway as a point man, if you have to raise your hand to stop us to correct a jam please do it. The point man can stop us for anything at any time, OK?", I asked. Smitty responded with, "That's a Roge".

"Now Mike, I don't know if you think you're John Wayne or something, but running up the trail and holding the gun above your shoulders while firing will cause you to be throwing lead all over the place, but hit very little", I said. "As slack-man your job is to cover the point-man, and that can best be done by keeping your weapon down and directly in front you in what we call the "Quick-Kill" position, like this", I said as I grabbed my 16 and demonstrated the position. "You will hit something quick like this as opposed to spraying bullets all over the place", I finished. "Also, standing or running completely upright as you were could get you drilled real quick, Roger?" "Roger he said.

"Ok, next I don't want to see any of you guys behind me, or anywhere, all bunched up without your interval. You make a big target like that, where either one bullet gets two or three, or this big of a target may make them use an RPG to get us all", I explained. "When walking down trails I want a five to ten foot interval between each man to avoid this, copy?" I asked. "Roger, copy, got it", were several responses given right back. "The more open the trail, the bigger the interval, and in thick jungle trails you'll need to close it up a bit to keep in visual contact with the guy in front of you", I explained.

"Terry and Jack, we need that gun on line and firing as quick as you can do it. Please do not get up and run the gun down an open trail. As fast as we need it doesn't mean we want you shot running up under fire. When contact happens in the future crawl or scurry on your knees if possible, but don't stand up. We want you around for a while, savvy?", I asked. "Roger that", Terry said. "Also, I didn't push you away from the gun because you weren't getting it to fire. M-60's are difficult to feed at times, and you always want your first belt in the gun while moving, but if it jams like it did today, I just knew some tricks from experience to get it going faster. I know how frustrating having trouble with a machine gun under fire can be, believe me", I said. "Once we got it firing, you did fine with it. Just make sure you keep it clean all of the time, and on firebases, cover it up with a towel to keep all of the dust the choppers stir up from gumming it up. Copy?" I asked. "Copy" was their reply.

"Over all you did well for your first fire-fight and I guess you know that this will give you a CIB", I told them. CIB's (Combat Infantrymen's Badge) was a coveted award for people in a war zone because it told people you have been in actual combat. It is also worn on all uniforms, including fatigues, that only jump wings and the CIB awards can be worn on. "We may not have killed any of the enemy, but anytime you can come out of a battle not hurt, it is a good day", I told them.

"All right, now is the time to get those weapons cleaned and your magazines reloaded. There is some more ammo over at the CP. Terry and Jack, clean that M-60 real well, and Jack if you have some belts of ammo that were on the ground, make sure to get a tooth brush and clean them off. You have all earned a good break, but first things first. We always have to be ready to go. Once all is together, relax with a break. I don't think we will be moving out again until the morning", I finished.

The next time out the CO sent me on a search mission for a new Lieutenant who had lost his platoon in the jungle while on patrol. Now in defense of the LT, triple canopy jungle is not very easy to navigate in, and he was pretty new at this. I took my squad out to what was the rendezvous point, but soon found that the LT wasn't able to find it. I checked my map again to make sure I was in the right place, and was sure that I was. Our maps were fairly accurate, and I had followed mine to where I was told he would be.

There were only eight of us and we had ventured out quite a way leaving us quite vulnerable to an attack. To make matters worse, the new LT had found the blue line (river) and was walking down it with his platoon, but was not where he thought he was. I knew if he just kept coming he would soon find us. I had the squad take up a defensive position on a ridge line looking over the river, which was narrower and more shallow than usual. This was lucky for the LT and his men because it made it much more easy to walk in it at only knee high.. The hot season had shrunk the river to about half its size which could be seen by the dried up water lines on both banks.

I contacted him on the radio and he wanted me to shoot in the air three times so he could head toward the noise. I told him, "Yeah, right, I'm going to fire in the air so the enemy can find us also. Forget it". Unfortunately, he being an officer ordered me to do it. I told him that we were just off the river on a ridge line in full view of the river so we could see him as he got near to us. "McBain fire the three shots and don't argue with me", was his quick response. I had the men to get down and take cover and I stood and fired in the air. As things turned out, the enemy did not find us, and the Lt. did, but not before ordering me to fire on two more occasions. It's a wonder incompetence like that doesn't get everyone killed, but we eventually made it back to the CP with the LT and his platoon intact.

One of things I did as a squad leader, and frankly was done by many of the squad leaders was not to put our men in harm's way for no reason. Most of us understood the futility of this war and that we were not going to be allowed to win it. Like Korea that the military learned very little from, we were again a policing action mainly used to keep the North Vietnamese Army and their cohorts, the Viet Cong out of the South and to stop them from developing the means to wage the war with the South Vietnamese.

Now we were all men who believed in Duty, Honor, and Country, but drew the line for extemporaneous crap the higher-ups kept coming up with. For instance, many of us squad leaders were sent on patrol in the jungle for no reason other than to keep us busy. The problem with that was putting men's lives at risk for patrols that had no objective or value. So I would take my squad out about two or three hundred yards from the platoon and tell them to sit down in a defensive perimeter. Once enough time had passed to reach the point we were to go to, I would call in to the CP and tell them we had reached our objective and had negative enemy contact. After enough time had passed for our return, we'd get up and walk back into the CP and no one was the wiser.

Now when we were in combat operations like this, usually several squads would be sent out to recon the area, but only one of those squads would be going in the direction that the platoon or company was moving in. If we were the squad that was moving the direction that the company was going to go, it was our duty to go all of the way and make sure we would find the enemy first if they were there. We always went on those occasions, and we always went all of the way if we didn't know which direction the whole group would later be moving in simply because it was the right thing to do.

Fortunately, we usually knew the direction the larger group was moving, and if we were sent another way, we would do our sit down. It never happened but I always realized if I were wrong and the company was going to move in the direction we were supposed to recon and didn't, that I'd have to confess to the CO what I had done. I was willing to take that chance, as were many of the other squad leaders, rather than go on a useless patrol and maybe get someone killed or wounded.

The next day I called my squad together and told them we were going out on a night ambush. I hated those but they were a part of life in the Nam. Again, because they had never been on a night ambush, I had to instruct them in what to take and not take on these night missions.

Here is a squad sized patrol that was typical for night ambushes. Very few brought their helmets, but instead wore Boonie hats. No rucksacks, but plenty of ammo, water, claymores, and trip flares with a poncho liner, and if raining, a poncho

"Ok guys take your weapons and plenty of ammo, one canteen on your pistol belts, and one claymore and trip flare each. Boonie hats if you have them will make you more comfortable, and leave any clanging junk with your ruck's here. Knives or bayonets can be helpful, but make sure your dog tags are under your shirt, and bring your poncho liners also". As we started out with now ten men, we went about a click and found a suspicious heap that did not look like it belonged there. I had the men hold up then told them to spread out and form a perimeter within sight of each other while I decided what we were going to do.

Finding caches of enemy weapons and materials was a mixed bag. It always felt good to destroy them, obviously so the enemy couldn't use them against us. Also, it was especially nice when you thought of the work of them having to hump all this heavy stuff down the Ho Chi Minh trail for hundreds of miles, just to find out it was discovered and destroyed when they came to get it. On the other hand, caches were dangerous many times as they could be booby-trapped to kill any finders if they messed with them. Unfortunately, there were numbers of soldiers that didn't think about that, or were just careless and paid a heavy price. I told the men to hold tight while I and another troop examined the site.

I didn't like the guys so spread out as they had to be to form a perimeter around this area, but as long as they could see each other there was enough daylight left to deal with this before it got too dark. I carefully approached the site and discovered a rather large piece of white metal that was covering it. The metal had been buried under a few inches of dirt, and they had thrown some brush over it. The brush may have tipped us off as it had turned brown and looked out of place, but what really got our attention was about a foot of the white metal had become uncovered and was easy to spot.

I called in to the CP and our platoon leader, call sign Troubled Waters One. "Troubled Waters One, Troubled

Waters One this is Troubled Waters Three, over". "Go ahead Three", said the LT. "Sir we have come upon what looks like a rather large cache, but have not discovered what all is in it, over", I said. "Three are you in a position to blow it in place", asked the LT. "Yes sir, however we have no C-4 with us unless we use claymores, over", I responded. There was a pause and then his reply,, "Ok, Do what you have to do to destroy it, Over", said the LT. "Roger One I copy destroy it, Over", I answered. "Roger three, Out".

I attached a cord to that corner of the metal that was showing, being careful not to disturb anything else. I got back about fifty feet letting out the cord as I went. After I made sure all of the men were down or far enough away, I jerked the cord hard and nothing happened. I then got up and pulled the metal cover off of the top of the hole, and moved up to take a look. What we had found was a good size cache of weapons and rockets. Chuck (the VC) must have really struggled to hump all of that stuff down the Ho Chi Minh trail and buried it for future attacks. "Sorry Charlie!"

Well I knew we had to blow it in place, but had no idea how large it was, or what all was in it. I ordered a couple of the guys to take their C-4 (plastic explosive) out of their claymores, which was usually a no-no, but we had no other choice, which was why the LT hesitated before telling me to go ahead. I carefully formed the pliable C-4 around a rocket. I attached an electrical blasting cap to the C-4, and ran some wire from there over the next little hill thinking that was plenty of distance. I had the squad move to the second little hill beyond me just to be sure they'd be Ok. I yelled fire in the hole three times, and then hit the firing device. When the C-4 blew it was like the whole earth shook.

Evidently, there was quite a bit more in that cache than appeared on the surface. There were hunks of metal and various materials raining down all over the place, and some even hit around where I was, but none went as far as where the men were. I was glad I had them move. After making sure all were Ok, I went back over the little hill I was behind, making sure there was no unexploded ordinance laying around. What I saw was an awesome sight. There was a gigantic hole blown in the earth that we could have driven a small car into. The CO and our LT couldn't help but hear the explosion a click away, and told us to come back in and forget the ambush, which was fine with me.

Night ambushes were a real pain because we rarely had the enemy cross our path in an ambush. It was hit or miss, and usually a miss. Mark Bogio, who came to us from the Big Red One when that division left Nam, and by the way was instrumental with his machine-gun in getting us pinned-downed guys off the ridge on Hill 882, told us of their unit using mechanical ambushes. A mechanical ambush (MA) was lining a trail with several claymore mines that were daisy-chained together to fire all at once. A PRC 25 radio battery was used as a power source to detonate the MA by being connected to a trip wire across the trail, which when tripped made the electrical connection that blew the claymores. These MA's could wipe out a whole squad if they were travelling in the right direction, where the point man hit the trip wire, and the rest of his squad was on the trail adjacent to the claymores.

We didn't use MA's in our unit and were told they were against the Geneva Convention. It always seemed unfair that we were expected to follow this convention's rules while the enemy was anything but conventional. A few days later, we moved to the top of a hill where an LZ had previously been blown to be resupplied. It was a very hot day and with the resupply came a replacement that the CO said would be in my squad. After packing up our rucksacks, the platoon moved out. The CO was moving with us today and my squad was bringing up the rear.

The replacement was a 20 year old redhead and a real problem. As my squad began to move off of the LZ into the jungle, this guy literally sat down and began to cry saying he couldn't carry his loaded rucksack in this heat. I told the men to move on with the platoon, and "Jeff" (Oliver Jefferson) stayed back with me to help me with this pathetic "Cherry". I tried at first to order him to get up and move out, but he wasn't going to do anything. I then felt compassion for him, even though he was just being a wimp.

I realized we were fooling around with him too long and that we were being separated from the platoon by an ever increasing distance. I told him to take his rucksack off and I threw it up on my shoulder by one strap while Jeff picked the kid up and helped him along. Fortunately, as always, I had my radio and called ahead to the LT to tell him of our situation. I was informed that they were not going to wait for us and that we had to catch up to them. I was very angry that this young man had put us in this situation and Jeff and I were worried about being separated from the main unit in this AO.

We did not catch up to the others until they had stopped to set up for the night, and it was a worrisome thing. I was so angry about this coward that when we got to the CP I took him by the arm and literally threw him down in front of the

CO and said, "I'm not taking this pussy in my squad, he's going to get someone killed". Much to my surprise the CO said OK, and actually had our squad take him back to the LZ the next morning and have him picked up and taken to the rear, where he was given a rear job. It really shocked me that the CO was doing this, and it was the first of any such thing I had ever see him do, but I was very glad he was doing it.

Sometime later when we were brought in to Camp Eagle for a stand-down, I saw this jerk in the enlisted men's bar drinking with a bunch of his friends and bragging about, "You just don't know how bad it is out there in combat", and telling other lies that never happened to him "out there". I couldn't keep from walking over to their table and saying, "Cherry, you weren't out there with us long enough to see anything happen before we had to ship your sorry ass in". He just lowered his head and kept silent until we left.

I hate to hurt people and feel I am as compassionate as the next guy, but this man was not only a coward, he was a liar that was spinning yarns of something he knew nothing about.

CHAPTER TWENTY

BATTALION RADIO OPERATOR

About a month later in early August 1970, a call came into our CP from the Battalion Commander, Col. Shay asking if I'd like to be one of his battalion radio operators in the battalion TOC (Tactical Operations Center). This meant I would be transferred to Headquarters Company, and serve out my remaining two months with Col. Shay on a fire base.

There was little thought given to my choice. Either stay in the "bush" in continual combat, or live on a firebase that is protected by a larger force, has hot food to eat, and work a somewhat regular shift. Even though a firebase is a sitting target for enemy mortars, rockets, and ground attacks, the perceived danger was by far less in my mind, and much more comfortable. Not only that, but I would be working directly for Col. Shay, who I believed to be a great battalion commander. He had just pinned the Bronze Star "V" on me a month or so prior in Camp Eagle. Although he never said so, I thought that is what prompted him to ask for me when one of his other RTO's went home. I decided to take the position and was thankful for it.

The Platoon Leader chose my replacement as Squad Leader, and I would be leaving in a few days. We were in a somewhat secure AO, and had not been moving much. However one of those days before I left, the FSB I would be going to, received a mortar attack on a bright, hot day, and then opened up on a slick coming in to the base with a fifty-caliber machine gun. They didn't shoot the chopper down, but the tracers were seen going right through the open doors. Unfortunately inside that chopper was one of my buddies, Willie Thomas who had come to the company the same day that I had. Willie was just returning from being wounded in the tank mine incident, and was the one across the road from me that yelled at me to stop because of a potential mine field.

As the chopper received that fire going in, they began to pull out to get away from that machine gun. As they turned, a round of that fifty caliber gun hit Willie in the leg, and wounded him again. I don't know just how bad it was because I never saw Willie again, but a fifty caliber bullet could easily take your leg right off. I was told he would be ok, but didn't find out in what regard that was meant. Would his leg heal, had he lost it, and how bad was it were questions I had, but never got an answer.

Saying good-bye to my guys was a little difficult, but they had only been with me a month and a half or so, and another seasoned squad leader was taking them, so I didn't worry much. Besides, I would be talking regularly with my old company on the battalion "push" (radio band), and be helping them with support operations like medevac's, artillery, cobra gunships, and supplies as they needed them.

"Pop smoke on the LZ", was the familiar sound I heard as the chopper sent to get me approached our location. I unstrapped my large Buck knife from my leg and handed it to the new squad leader. "You're gonna need this more than me", I said. As I ran out to the chopper, and threw my rucksack on it. I turned for a last wave good-bye, gave a thumbs-up, and jumped on the chopper heading for my new job. "Strike Force", I yelled over the chopper noise as we began to lift off. "Airborne", yelled several of my men back to me. I sat on the edge of the door, with my feet on the chopper skid as we lifted into the air. Slowly I moved

Chopper leaving a LZ in the jungle after dropping off and picking up. The enemy was not near as can be seen by the guys all standing in the open

myself back further on the chopper floor, thinking about the last nine months in country, and the horrors I'd witnessed, as well as the fun I had at times.

Once I landed on the FSB, I reported in to the XO, Major Kite who was on duty in the TOC. He introduced me to a couple of the other RTO's on duty then, and sent me to find a Sergeant who would show me my living place. It was a four-man hooch built with a combination of artillery ammo boxes, sandbags, and a metal culvert for a roof covered with a double layer of sandbags. I had the rest of the day off and was to report to the TOC in the morning. I walked around recognizing some of the guys who had been in the boonies with us for a time until they got called for duty of one kind or another on the fire base. I ran into an old friend named Tolliver who would eventually teach me some guitar lessons.

The next morning I reported to the TOC bright and early,

and the guys there began showing me the different radios, and explaining the TOC SOP when the units hit combat or called for something. I settled right in and began with the simple sit-reps to the companies. The next week on the job training was very helpful. Watching what the others did, and how they handled the different situations as they came in was most instructive. It was so different and so nice to work regular hours, as I had never had them as long as I had been in the Army. Then of course, the regular hot chow was a real treat, and I really caught up with both of my letter writing and book reading, with some guitar lessons in between on someone else's guitar.

One of the guys in the TOC had been with my company in the field for a while like I had been. I recognized him but didn't know him because he was in another platoon. He showed me how to use the "Secure" as we called it, which scrambled the communications between that radio and another "Secure". All regular radios could not decipher these transmissions.

The TOC was either hectic or boring, depending on the day, and enemy contact if any made by the companies in the bush. On one occasion, Col. Shay was off duty and asleep, while his XO was on duty, and supposed to be in the TOC. My old company had made heavy contact, and they were in a serious firefight with an enemy force. They called in while I was on duty and needed Medevac's and Cobra's for support.

"Where's Major Kite", I yelled to others in the TOC. "Out walking the hill", someone said. "Damn it, he's supposed to be in here...see if you can find him", I angrily said. The officer on duty had to give the orders to call in Medevac's and Cobra Gunships. I was getting very angry that the

Major was not near the TOC in this tense situation. The man came back and said he couldn't find the XO.

The calls became urgent from my old buddies, and I decided to step out on a limb. "Cobra Striker, Cobra Striker, this is Shamrock Alpha One, over", I called to the chopper center. "Go ahead One, over", they responded. "Cobra Striker I need two Smoke-Bringers (Cobra Gunships) and a Dust-off (Medevac), over", I said. "Roger", they said in return, "Where do you need them"? they asked. "Coordinates Charlie three fiver at Foxtrot two niner, and be advised that Razor's Edge is in contact with two down, and the LZ is red, Copy?" I stated. "Roger Alpha One, we copy and are on our way, over". "Roger Cobra Striker, what is your ETA (estimated time of arrival) over", I asked? "Alpha One our ETA is one zero mikes, Copy, over?" they answered. "Roger that Cobra Striker, Alpha One out".

I then called to the company CP's RTO. "Tanner One, Tanner One, Shamrock Alpha One, over." "Mac is that you?" was asked by the RTO, and I could hear firing in the back ground. "Roger Tanner One, smoke-bringers and dust-off is inbound to your location; ETA is eight mikes, copy, over", I told him. "Copy Shamrock Alpha, Thanks, out". When the Cobra's got there with the Medevac, I turned the command and control over to the CO of my old company. About that time, Major Kite came back to the TOC and started yelling at me.

"Now McBain...McBain, what are you doing...what's going on here...you can't call in support without my authorization... what's going on here?", he ranted. I replied, "Sir, my company hit heavy contact and needed a Medevac and Cobra's, and you weren't here where you belonged...

we looked for you and couldn't find you and I wasn't going to waste time and let these guys die while we waited for you to show up, Sir". "Now, now McBain, you can't do this, you can't do this, and I'll have you court martialed. I'm going to report this to the Colonel because you can't do this", he said, and started out of the TOC.

Major Kite seemed like a nice man usually, but a bit squirrely. He was a thin, short man with a high pitched voice that reminded me a great deal of Barney Fife in the Andy Griffith TV series back home. Just as he moved away to get the Colonel, Shamrock walked into the TOC. "Sir, McBain broke SOP, and called in gunships and a Medevac", he started. He knows he's not authorized to do that, and I think…" Col. Shay put up his hand to stop him, and walked over to me. "What's going on Mac", he asked?

"Sir, Alpha Company hit heavy enemy contact and called for Cobra's and a Medevac. The XO was out of the TOC and I sent someone to find him but they didn't. I knew what to do and I did it, Sir", I explained. There was nothing said by anyone in the TOC for about thirty seconds. "OK Mac, you did fine, carry on", he said. "Yes sir", I snapped back in the proper military fashion. "Major I'd like to see you outside", Shamrock said. I never heard another word about it, and the XO never left the TOC again while on duty.

Since I had to work under Major Kite's command also, I was hoping he would get past this incident and not hold it against me. One morning he came in and sat down next to me and asked, "Mac, where are you from?" I could see he was trying to break the ice and clear the air. "Dayton, Ohio sir", I responded. We went on making conversation about family and what we did before the Army, and from then on we were fine with each other.

One evening about two hours before it would be dark, the CO came and got me and told me to bring my M-16, ammo, and my pistol belt with a canteen of water and come to the TOC. He said it in a hushed manner close to my ear so no one else would hear it. I got up, grabbed my rifle and a canteen and caught up with him on the way back to the TOC. Outside the TOC were standing a few men looking like civilians but dressed in some other type of jungle fatigues. It turns out they were CIA men. We went to the chopper pad, and I was carrying a secure radio that scrambled messages. On board the chopper was a sort of box looking device, about the size of a camper refrigerator. No one was talking and so I just sat back and enjoyed the ride.

We flew into the sunset to a location I was told was near the Laotian Border. This was going to be a test of a new radio beacon air strike that was being developed. I have no idea how it worked, but I was told that theoretically this equipment that the other men brought, would beacon to a B-52 bomber and provide a target to drop on.

I was told to call the pilots of the B-52 aircraft. When they answered I told them to hold, and handed the horn to the CO. Col. Shay was speaking to them and using some code words I had not heard before. (If I told you, I would have to kill you, LOL). I then took back the handset of the secure radio and spoke to the B-52 pilots only what I was told to say and they eventually dropped a load of bombs. When they acknowledged the mission was done, there was almost nothing said except "Let's Go". We then hurriedly packed up and flew back to the FSB. The next morning I heard that the bombs had been dropped about twenty-two miles off target. Of course they purposely did not target anything but a spot in the jungle because this was an early test of this equipment, and they weren't sure how it would work. I got the idea that they were disappointed that it had not worked better, but I never heard any more about it.

Duty in the TOC could be nerve-racking, especially when the companies in the bush made contact with the enemy. On my headset I could hear the gunfire, explosions, the screams, and frantic orders being yelled to the combatants by their officers, while their RTO's were calling in their needs. Having been in combat for over nine months myself, vivid pictures roamed through my head as I heard all of these same things from afar instead of right there. It gave me mixed feelings of being glad I wasn't there anymore, but also a feeling like I should be running to the fight to help my brothers.

Listening carefully through all of this was key in doing the best I could to help them out. "Shamrock" was almost always there directing us what to tell the RTO's, and directing us to call in Phantoms or Cobras or both, and medevac's when needed. While contact was going on, chaos could take over if we let it. It was our duty to remain calm so we could get our critical work done, but also to sound reassuring to those fighting for their lives, and encouraging them that the "World" was on its way to destroy the enemy.

Listening to the responders was always very interesting as they came on push. Some of the comments, which were not SOP, were fun to hear when the pilots took to helping the ground forces win the battle. Some of the typical things you might hear during these engagements were: "Ok two-niner, I see five little bastards trying to flank you from the north about twenty-meters from your pos, (position) over". "Roger Cobra-five". Then the sound of the Cobra's mini-guns. "That's five dead little gooks two-niner", said the pilot. "I'm going to take care of that ridge-line to your west. Are there any friendlies over there?" he asked. "Wait one, Seven Alpha, Seven Alpha, how close are you to the ridgeline, over" was asked by two-niner. "Two-niner this is Seven-Alpha, our lead element's proximity is thirty meters back east of the ridge-line, over", came the response. "Well get your heads down, copy?" Roger, copy that Two-niner".

"Cobra-five our guys are 30 meters east of the ridge-line, over". "Roger two-niner, rolling in". The Cora gunships would pull up into a steep climb when attacking, and turn and dive on their targets. The sight was awesome but made you glad it was not coming toward you. As the Cobra dove he fired multiple rockets, sheew, sheew, sheew, sheew, followed by miniguns with their r-r-r-r-r-r-r-r-r- loud roar, then boom, boom, boom, boom as the rockets hit. Miniguns fired 4,000 rounds per minute thus the roar, and killed anything in their path.

Two-niner we have a clear ridgeline, over", the pilot said as he passed over the target area. "Roger, copy that Cobra-five, and great shooting, thanks!" was the CO's reply. Now situations like these were common as we covered the whole Battalion operating in four companies and a Recon Platoon. The companies were usually broken up operating in platoon size, and even squad size at times.

One of the benefits of TOC duty was that we could do almost anything we wanted when off duty, including catching a chopper back to the base camp, with permission, to pick up something for ourselves or for the Colonel. A week or so later, after the secret mission, I caught a chopper back to our base camp, and bought a cheap guitar in a "gook shop". Back on the firebase I had a buddy who played guitar and began to show me some chords. I wanted to have my own guitar so I could practice what he showed me without having to find him and borrow his guitar. The first song I ever played was "Sounds of Silence" by Simon & Garfunkle. It was a good pastime for my off duty hours.

This firebase was no different from any firebase, and we had our occasional mortar attack. Thank God we never had a ground attack while I was there. My first CO, who was also a Green Beret, was in a ground attack shortly after leaving our company and joining the Battalion CP on FSB Rifle. He had been hurt pretty bad in the attack when the sappers threw a satchel charge into the CP while he was in there. That firebase was a mess after the attack, and back when it happened, we were moved back on rifle to help

Destruction of FSB Rifle after a Sapper attack overran the base. My first CO was a Green Beret that was almost killed in this attack when a Sapper threw a satchel charge into the CP (Command Post) while he was in there

clean it up.

Most everyone was excited to get their "Short-Timers Calendar". This was a one page calendar we would keep usually when we'd get 30 to sometimes 60 days out from finishing our tour of duty and going home. It was a special thing to us to have one as it meant you were "Short" and of course were given the title, "Short-Timer".

They had different pictures on them, but mine had a big picture of Snoopy, flying his Sopwith Camel dog house. Mine had little squares starting at the top with the number 30, and counting down to Zero – It's over. We looked forward to every day being able to "X" out the appropriate square. People would ask, "How many days short are you?" You were always happy to give that number out because you liked to keep hearing it yourself.

CHAPTER TWENTY-ONE

A HUGE SURPRISE

My DEROS date (date eligible for return from overseas) was November 10th, 1970. I had been marking my thirty day Short-Timers Calendar which now had about twelve days crossed off of it. It was a treat to mark off every day knowing you were very close to going home, but also scary as I had seen too many "Short-timers "get it" before their time was up.

It seemed like each of us became paranoid the shorter we got. It was a real challenge to keep my mind off of what could still happen, instead of the joy of knowing you were almost there. I tried to fill my off duty time with playing guitar, reading, writing letters, and talking with the guys about positive things.

With a day over two weeks to go something totally unexpected happened. This day was October 25th, and I was just coming on duty when I had one of the best surprises of my life. Lt.Col. Shay came up to me and said, "What are you doing here Dick, you're leaving today". "Going where, Sir", I asked? "Home Mac, Home; back to the world", he replied. "I got you a two week early out, so get your stuff together ASAP", he said smiling.

I could hardly contain my surprise and excitement. "Yes Sir, thank you Sir, you don't have to tell me twice", I exclaimed as I started to run out of the TOC. "Oh Mac, I'm sending you in to Camp Eagle in my Charlie-Charlie Bird so hurry up", he said almost laughing at me falling all over myself, trying to decide what to do first.

I ran to my hooch yelling to anyone I saw, "I'm outta here". Many of the guys came up to my hooch in surprise. "Are you kidding, Dick...You going home...How'd you swing that...I thought you had two more weeks or so", the questions came from several of my buddies, who had been keeping up with my daily "Short-timers countdown.

"Two week early out...back to world....'outta this hellhole", I said back to them, as I grabbed my rucksack, rifle, guitar, and ammo. "Ok, who will learn to play the guitar if I leave it with you?" I asked as I was still going through things I didn't need to take with me. "I will", said one of the guys who had just been there a few days. I didn't know him but he was the only one to speak up so I said, "Ok, it's all yours". I handed him the guitar I had bought in the rear, which was a pretty cheap "Gook- made" guitar, but it certainly was good enough to learn on, as I could testify to.

I kept looking for things I could give away that others might need, but of course couldn't give away Army issued items as I had to turn them in or be charged for them. When I got through giving away what I could, I simply said, "Ok, gotta go, good luck to you all", and then ran for the chopper pad. The "Charlie-Charlie Bird" was starting its engine when I got to it.

As I ran to the chopper pad a number of my friends were there waiting to say good-bye. "Shamrock" was instructing the pilot about something, and a couple of the guys were taping on smoke grenades to the chopper skids. This was done usually on special occasions, and I was pleased they thought this was one of them; I sure did!

There were handshakes and "the pound" given all around as I jumped on the chopper. The smoke grenades popped as we began to lift off, and I hung out of the door yelling "Strike Force...see ya back in the world", to my buddies as the chopper turned for Camp Eagle and we flew away.

It was a great feeling as we approached Camp Eagle, and I thought this is the last time I will ever have to go up or down all these stairs to the chopper pad. I thanked the chopper pilot and jumped off the bird then realizing this would probably be the last helicopter ride of my life.

As I began my descent down the many steps to the company area, I thought about how I had ridden on just about every kind of chopper there was in Vietnam, and loved them all, except the Chinook, which most of us called, "Shithook" . They were the long, double-bladed work horse of the Army, and could carry thirty-three troops in jump seats. It was also the chopper used to deliver heavy equipment like artillery guns and even jeeps. I didn't like the Chinooks mostly because they were big targets, and would move up and down in big jumps when hovering, and you couldn't see where you were going.

I stopped for a moment in front of our orderly room. It all seemed very strange to me that this nightmare was really coming to an end. It's hard to explain the feeling I had when for a year I wasn't at all sure whether or not I was going to make it out of the Nam alive, and especially well. As it began to sink in that I would be home in a couple of days, I began to get excited, and headed up the stairs to the office.

"Top, I'm going home", I said as I arrived in the company orderly room. "Yeah, I know you lob cock" he replied

Chinook 47 – Delivering a container to a fire support base. These choppers were the workhorse of the infantry carrying ammo, jeeps, artillery pieces to where they were needed. They also could carry up to forty-four troops, and had machine guns in the windows

breaking a smile. "You can go ahead and start your equipment turn-in now, and take these forms with you, and make sure they're initialed by each station you report to", he said handing me forms he had started for me. "That is unless you want to re-up", he smirkingly said. "No thanks, Top...seven more months and I'm out of the green machine for good", I said while running out of the door.

I had been told that two weeks ago the 101st had sent a comical letter to my folks which read the following way:

ISSUED IN SOLEMN WARNING, this day of 7 October, 1970

To the family, relatives, friends, neighbors, and civil authorities of S/4 Richard L. McBain:

1. Very soon the above named individual will again be in your midst, DE-AMERICANIZED, DEMORALIZED, DECIVILIZED, AND DEHYDRATED. There will be many subtle changes which have resulted from his overseas tour. We hope that this paper will serve as a guide in rehabilitating and retraining him for life "back in the world."

2. In making joyous preparations to welcome him back into a respectable society, you must make allowances for the crude environment in which he has suffered for the past twelve months. In a word, he may be somewhat ASIATIC. He is probably suffering from Viet-Congitis or too much Ba-Maui-Ba beer.

3. Show no alarm if he prefers to squat rather than sit on the couch, or wanders about outside clad only in thong sandals and towel, slyly offering to sell cigarettes to passers-by. Just be understanding when he picks and picks at his food suspiciously as if you're trying to poison him. Don't be surprised if he answers questions with, "I hate this place" or "Number 10". Be tolerant when he tries to buy everything at less than the marked price, accuses the grocer of being a thief, and refuses to enter establishments or buses that don't have steel meshed screens over the doors and window.

4. Inform him that the entire bathroom is his from now on, and that it's inside. He may be incredulous at the sight of a flush toilet, so show him how to operate it, and don't be upset if he just stands there flushing and flushing with a stunned expression on his face.

5. For the first few months (until he is home broken) be especially watchful when he is in the company of women,

particularly young, beautiful specimens. Try to limit the number of women to only one or two at a time, for too much at once might trigger a near convulsive state. The staring, drooling, and mumbling should subside in a few weeks. Wives and sweethearts are advised to take advantage of this…….

6. You'll find it helpful to flatter him occasionally by asking him to expound on the qualities of ten different kinds of Japanese cameras, and show you his Seiko watch.

7. Be tolerant when it rains and he runs outside with a bar of soap, strips naked and takes a shower. Be aware that when he hears a backfire or a siren he may begin to yell incoming. Dissuade him if he wants to go on patrol through the neighborhood while looking for his rifle.

8. In closing, get a full tank of gas, load the refrigerator with plenty of beer and steaks, hide the hunting rifles, and keep the women off the streets, because the kid is coming home!

When I got to S-4 to turn my weapon and gear in, I ran into a problem with the Sergeant at the front desk. He said, "This is not your weapon, this has a different serial number than the M-16 you were issued. Unless you turn in the right weapon, you will have to pay two hundred and fifty dollars for your weapon".

Now I tried to keep my cool but this "REMF" (rear echelon mother f'er), a term we used of the jerky rear people was ticking me off with his smug attitude toward a fellow soldier who had been in the jungle in combat for the last year.

"Sergeant", I began, "You take this weapon and sign my paper, or you and I are going to have a problem", I said. "I can't give you credit for turning in the wrong weapon", he tried to explain. "Where is the weapon you were issued? he asked. I wanted to explain to him but I was getting too mad to talk to him. "Go get me the S-4", I said very angrily. He could see I was getting hostile and decided he better do what I asked. He went in the back and came out with the S-4 officer.

This Captain was a West Pointer and we had become friendly when I was in the rear after my medevac. We struck up a conversation when I was at S-4 to pick something up, and talked about West Point, and me going to Miami University and other personal stories. During our talk he had offered me some Screaming Yellow Zonkers, which I had never heard of, that he had received in a package from home. They were some kind of buttery caramel coated popcorn that tasted great.

The Captain recognized me and said, "hey man, how you doing?" I answered, "great sir, I'm going home tomorrow, that is if this Sergeant will stop playing big shot with me. The Captain looked at his Sergeant then at me and said, "What do you mean?" "Sir, instead of taking a helpful approach to a year-long combat trooper, he emphatically and smugly said he would not sign my sheet for this weapon. The Sergeant quickly responded, "Sir this is not the weapon he was issued. It's another serial number".

"Captain as you may remember, I was medevac'd off Hill 882, where my M-16 had been burned up while I was pinned down and surrounded for 25 minutes. And after I was blown up by a satchel charge, I took my Lieutenant's M-16 as he was dying, and began to fire that. I was later brought in still having the Lieutenant's weapon, while mine lay somewhere in the jungle, burned up and unusable".

"Yes, yes I remember! Sergeant, take this weapon, record the serial number as this man's, and sign his sheet. Specialist McBain You have a safe trip home, and be careful", said the Captain. "Thank you sir", I replied.

I went to Records to get my DEROS orders, and found I had the regular thirty-day leave before I had to report to Ft. Riley, Kansas and the Big Red One (First Infantry Division) for my last seven months in the Army. I returned to the company orderly room. "What do I do now, Top", I asked? "Well you have till day after tomorrow so you need to stay here at least tonight, and tomorrow you can stay here or go to Phu Bai where you catch a plane to Cam Rahn Bay the next morning", he replied. "Thanks Top", I said.

I left the orderly room and found some of my friends who had received rear jobs. That night I was with Doc Shenk and a couple of other buddies and we "partied hardy". I was celebrating and got both drunk and stoned on grass. About 11:00 hours we were in Doc's hooch when all of the lights went out and sirens started signaling a ground attack. I went into a pure panic as I had already turned my rifle in and could not find my way out of the hooch in the complete darkness. There were dividers up separating the beds from each other, and I kept running into these makeshift walls.

Doc finally found me and led me outside where we were about to look for some cover when the sirens stopped and the lights came on, and the all clear was given. It turned out to be a false alarm, and I was not amused. I had finally been able to relax for a while until this scenario once again brought extreme tension.

"Hooch's" in our rear area at Camp Eagle were quarters for the rear staff personnel, both sleeping areas and Orderly Rooms. They were sandbagged about five feet up the sides in case of rocket attack. When we came in from the jungle, tents would be put up in the area with ditch's dug for cover

The next morning my old company was in for a stand-down. Sergeant Johnson found me and told me to come with him. He and Doc Shenk had troubled themselves getting together my decorations for my dress uniform and the trip home. I put on my new khaki uniform and Doc put the blue infantry cord on my shoulder. Then Sergeant Johnson pulled out the three ribbon base, and began sliding the ribbons in it. He explained to me the order they needed to be in so I'd know. "Ok Mac, the top row you put to the left the two bronze stars which is one ribbon with an oak leaf cluster and a "V" device in the middle of the ribbon, and next to it the purple heart", he explained. "Next row, from left to right, the Army Commendation ribbon, Air Medal ribbon, and Good Conduct ribbon. Then, last row Vietnam Service ribbon, Vietnam Campaign ribbon, and the National Defense ribbon. After he had slid all of the ribbons on in order he pinned on my three rows of ribbons and said remember the order they are in. Next they handed me a new CIB which I put on, then he pinned on the navy blue Presidential Unit Citation. These guys were very close buddies of mine and I knew I was going to miss them.

The next afternoon I told the First Sergeant that I was going to Phu Bai for this last night, especially after the last night's debacle. "OK", Top said, "Just sign out of the company roster here, and catch a truck going over there". "Top, I"... "I know kid, we'll miss you too, now get outta here before I put you on guard duty', he said with a smile. I ran out on the main drag and flagged a deuce and a half (truck) down to get a ride to Phu Bai. I met an old friend, Joe Mazza there who had come over to Vietnam with me. We had been friends in infantry training, and now we were going home together. Joe had been in the 101st, but assigned to another battalion, so I had only seen him once or twice during our tour in the Nam.

"Hey Joe, I see you decided not to stay at Camp Eagle tonight either", I said as I saw him. "Yeah, they can't mess with us in Phu Bai," he replied. "Well how the heck are you doing?" I asked. "Probably the same as you, happy to be getting the hell out of the Nam alive and in one piece", he said. "So you got an early out also", I stated as he and I had flown over on the same plane. "Yeah, a great surprise I gotta say", he commented. Joe and I found the nearest enlisted man's bar and began to tie one on. That night we talked about our battles, and who we both knew that had been killed. Gary Manchester had flown over with us, and was killed in the first month. Mike Walsh had also flown over with us, but was wounded bad enough to get sent home early.

We later snuck into a plane hangar to crash, and we leaned

up against our duffel bags in the hangar at the air base in Phu Bai. About two o'clock in the morning, the explosions of rockets hitting Camp Eagle, some six miles away, awakened us. Later we got through to our battalions, and found out that the rockets had hit my company area, where I would have been had I stayed the night in Camp Eagle. I was glad I had not. No one we knew was injured, so we went back to sleep.

The next morning, we climbed into the back of a C-130 bound for Cam Rahn Bay. It was rainy and windy and we were told the flight would take an hour and a half or so. The plane was getting thrown around by turbulent's and after about forty-five minutes or so we started to go down…fast! I looked at my watch and told Joe, "We can't be there yet; it's been only forty-five minutes". It literally felt like we were falling from the sky, but when looking to the Air Force crew, no one seemed rattled. Just then we came out under the cloud ceiling and could see the ground. The pilot came on and said, "Sorry for that guys, we caught a huge tailwind and got here much earlier than expected." We could have cared less by then as we could now at least see the air base, and we landed without further incident.

Cam Rahn Bay looked about the same as a year ago when I was coming in country and put on guard duty, but obviously the feeling was now joyous with a year of combat behind me instead of facing me. Now it was me going home while others were coming in. Now it was me walking down the road with my year behind me and a CIB above my left pocket.

As we walked down the road to chow I decided to be different to the new guys than the old-timers had been to me. I could see the fear on the faces of these men coming in with a year ahead of them. I asked the same question that was asked of me a year ago, "What's your MOS?" To those who responded Eleven Bravo I didn't hang my head and walk away silently, but would stop and ask if they knew their unit assignment yet. Whatever they told me, I would try and cheer them up with, "Oh that's a great unit, you'll be fine", or something like that.

We were at Cam Rahm overnight for out-processing from the country, and then we were taken to the Air Force Base. At the base they took us into a room off the tarmac and gave us a debriefing. The main purpose was to make it clear that anyone trying to take out weapons or Army materials not specifically issued, in other words, contraband, would be detained and not go home. The same applied with drugs of any kind. They explained that when we got up and started out the door, we would enter a small building, one at a time which was an "Amnesty Room". There were bins on both sides of the isle that we would be in where no one could see, and we could deposit any contraband into those bins and no questions would be asked. Once we came out on the other side, if we were searched and caught with any contraband, we would not be leaving, and even possibly brought up on charges.

This scared me because any thought of not getting out of there now was unimaginable to me. Now I had been given as a gift a brand new pair of Jungle Boots, but they were Army issue and I shouldn't have them. When I got in the Amnesty Room, I quickly opened my duffel bag, and took the boots out putting them into a bin. I then proceeded out and saw that no one was searching anyone, and many of the guys were taking contraband home with no care. I felt a little wimpy! After an out processing there, we boarded a Pan American jet (freedom bird), and waited for takeoff.

There were always rumors that the VC would try and blow up planes with mortar's that were waiting for clearance on the runway taking GI's home.

Unfortunately, we had taxied out for takeoff, and were being held up due to some custom's slip-up. We all began to get extremely anxious as we just sat waiting at the end of the runway, for what seemed to be an eternity. Finally, the plane began to move forward. All of the soldiers aboard began rocking in their seats, saying, C'mon...C'mon... C'mon", as the plane moved faster and faster down the runway. The plane lifted off the ground, and all hell broke loose. Soldiers were grabbing the flight attendants and kissing them; pillows began flying around the cabin; shouts from everyone exploded, and I sat back and took a deep breath, thanking God I would never step foot in Vietnam again.

Troops going home loading on a "Freedom Bird", the name given to the planes that were taking us home

CHAPTER TWENTY-TWO

HOME FROM VIETNAM

The flight home was about ten hours, with a stopover in Japan. We left Vietnam at about two o'clock in the afternoon, and landed in Japan a few hours later. Once back in the air we knew it would be a long flight to the U.S., and tried to settle in to get some rest. I laid my head back and wondered what might be in store on the home front. Obviously before I left for Vietnam, and certainly during my tour of duty, most news was about the unrest in the United States and especially on the campuses.

Demonstrations seemed everywhere, and being that we did not have access to instant and continual news as we have today, most of what we heard was very negative. We also had news of the bad treatment of returning soldiers from hippies and the anti-war protesters calling names like baby-killer, murderer, and the like even in the airports before they managed to get home. We had our own people having these horrific things happen to them

I remember hearing about one of our Sergeants who landed in New York and was on his way home to see his parents. Before he got home, while he was walking along a street in his neighborhood, a group of long-hairs surrounded him and were calling him all these terrible names. He lost his temper and grabbed one of them and hit him knocking him into the corner of a brick building. Unfortunately he was killed from the impact, and our Sergeant was arrested on the spot and taken to jail before he even got home to see his folks.

Many Vietnam vets were returning home to find people

against them, who did not want to hear about their experiences, and learning of a self-serving political machine that didn't seem to care either. In our discussions on the way home, Joe Mazza and I told each other of some of these stories we had heard and remembered our trip over one year ago.

"Hey Joe last year when we were flying over, we had Gary Manchester with us and Walsh, and we all said we'd be flying back together this year", I began. These were buddies all the way from basic training through infantry training and flew over with us to the Nam. "Gary was killed only four or five weeks later walking point for his unit when a gook with an RPG popped up and cut him in two with it", I related. "Yea, and Mark Walsh was hit about six months into his tour and shipped home wounded", Joe added. "Just think of the innocence of us back then", I continued, "well trained but not really understanding what it was actually going to be like until the guns opened up". "Lord God I'm glad this is over for us", I stated.

Joe Mazza and I discovered we were both being reassigned to Ft. Riley, Kansas after our leaves. We both were assigned to the Big Red One, but different companies. We were pleased that we would at least be in a close proximity, and able to pal around together when we reported to the base. "Hey Joe, you headed to New Guernsey tomorrow", I asked, remembering how we joked about his home state of New Jersey when we were in training? "Yeah, going back to the block to beat the crap out of Jody for stealing the girlfriend I never had", he said laughing. "Jody" was the military's proverbial name for the guy who would take your wife or girlfriend while you were away doing your duty.

It was still dark outside the airplane, and we settled back to get a couple of more hours of sleep before arriving in Seattle. I began to think about getting back into college once I got out of the Army, and started to recall how I ended up in the Army when I should have had a college deferment. The fault was mine based on my own immaturity and playing around instead of studying.

"Dick, Dick we're coming into McCord", Joe said as he shook me with a sense of excitement. "McCord", I said slowly, then I realized what that meant, McCord Air Force Base, and sat up quickly, "All right, we made it"! The Pan Am "freedom bird" touched down, and once again, all hell broke loose. We were home...back in the world....the good ole' USA. It was dark outside and must have been around Ten pm. We made our way to the door, and started down the stairs to the ground. A number of armed Air Force guards were at the bottom of the stairway. Joe and I hit the ground, fell to our knees, and kissed the ground as many of the other guys were doing. We jumped up and grabbed a guard or two and started dancing around while they looked at us as the typical nutty returnees from the Vietnam.

We were led inside for a debriefing, and told we would be taken to Ft. Lewis by bus for new dress uniforms and preparation for our trips to our individual homes. I went to find a phone to call home and let them know I was in the USA safely. My family had no idea that I got out of Vietnam two weeks early, and thought I was still there. It was now about midnight, making it three am at home. I dialed the old familiar number, and it rang a few times until I heard my mother's voice say, "Hello". "Hi Mom, it's Dick", I said excitedly. "Dick...Dick...are you OK...what's happened?" she asked expecting something was wrong. "I'm home Mom, I'm in Seattle and I'll be home tomorrow", I said quickly trying to dispel her fears. "Seattle...home...but I thought you had a couple of weeks more", she said unbelievingly. "Hello Son", my Dad said as he picked up another extension. "Hi Dad, I'm Home and will be there tomorrow", I repeated to bring him up to speed.

"Mom, I got a two week drop in my time, and we just got here at Ft. Lewis a little while ago", I said. My mother started crying, and said, "Oh thank God you're ok and almost home; I can't believe it"! "You say you're going to be here tomorrow?" Dad asked. "Well, really today since its already early morning", I answered. "I'm getting my uniform now, then I shoot to Sea-Tac airport to catch a plane home", I continued. "I'll have to call you when I know what airline and what time I'll arrive in Dayton, but if all goes well, I should be there this afternoon", I said.

"Oh I can't believe it", my mother said excitedly. "I gotta' go now but I'll call as soon as I know", I said. "OK son, we'll be waiting for your call", Dad said as I quickly said good-bye and hung up the phone. I couldn't wait to see my folks, but I first had to focus on getting processed out. In Vietnam, Sergeant Johnson had gathered and put together my medals and ribbons, so when I got my uniform, which was tailored on the spot, it was quick and easy to get all the ribbons in place. I had three rows of ribbons which were a bit unusual for a guy who had only been in a year and a half. I was given the Blue Infantry Braid to wear over my shoulder, and looked like an overdone Christmas tree.

I hurriedly signed out on leave, and caught a military bus to Sea-Tac airport where I signed up for military stand-by, and was told I was on a United Flight to Chicago leaving at eleven am, then continuing on to Dayton, arriving at three thirty pm. It would be several hours until my flight left, so I called home again to give them the times, and then I found a nice airport bench to crash on.

I watched the returning vets as they walked through the airport wondering if I would see any of that protester crap we had been told about, but I saw none. I saw some long-hairs or hippies once in a while but none that hassled any of the military guys. I have to admit it seemed strange to now be in an American airport after only hours ago being in a combat zone for so long. I could tell it would take a little time to readjust to a life I had in what seemed to be years ago. I was so happy not to have to worry about killing or being killed anymore that I was more than up to making the adjustment.

After landing in Chicago, a stewardess came up to me and asked if I was returning from Vietnam. I said that I was, and she said she was moving me to the first class section of the airplane. I remember thinking how nice that was of her, and as I got to my seat, there were a number of businessmen around me, drinking and wanting me to tell them about Nam. They continued to buy me drinks while I spun my yarns, and thank God the flight was only an hour and a half. When we landed in Dayton, I was "lit up", and almost tripped down the stairs of the plane. There at the bottom of the stairs were my Mom and Dad, my sister Gail and her husband Mike, with Tommy their son, and my sister Ginny. My brothers were both away in the Army; John was still in Washington, and Bob was in Germany. This was one of the happiest days in my life.

As we pulled into our driveway, a banner was hanging over the front of the garage which said, "Welcome Home Hero". My Dad had put that up, and I found out that the local

Dick coming off plane (first in the middle of walkway) in Dayton, Ohio half loaded with First Class businessmen buying drinks. Waiting on the tarmac were my Mom, Dad, sister Gail, husband Mike, and nephew Tommy. Pictured here were Mom, Dad, Dick, and Tommy

newspaper had run a picture of me receiving the Bronze Star "V" and the citation with it.

Some of the neighbors saw us arrive and came over. The neighbors and friends I knew wanted to hear all about the war, and discuss political views, both positive and negative about Vietnam. Because of this, I was able to readjust quickly and safely by being enabled to dump the trauma and stress from the fear I had lived with for almost a year.

To me, there was a big difference between being against the war, which I was, and the idiots who maligned our soldiers for doing their sworn duty. Demonstrating against the war was fine with me, but the demonstrators should have realized that most of the soldiers in Vietnam didn't want to be there. Most of us went because our country called, and we knew we would have nothing but anarchy if everyone got to decide whether they would serve or not when their country went to war. We were all afraid, but the

Dick in uniform at home, and he had been gone less than a year and a half from civilian life, and now had to readjust from the horrors he had witnessed. He still had seven months left to serve

cowards who hid behind student movements were the scum of the earth to me.

I personally felt we had no business being in Vietnam, and even thought of joining Vietnam Vet's Against the War after I returned. I never did, but was very infuriated that our government would not let us win that war. I am a Patriot, and believe we have a duty to repay when called, whether we agree or not. Very few people wanted anything to do with World War II at first, but later realized it was necessary. Vietnam turned out to be anything but necessary. It was a terrible waste of life, but the country had made the decision to be there, and we had to aspire to the higher calling of serving our country instead of selfish interests.

Although it felt good to be home, it took some getting used to. Just to have hot meals every day, and be able to come and go as I pleased seemed strange. It was late October of 1970, and I was ever conscious of my short hair wherever I went. Long hair was the style, and people could spot military men easily. I decided that I had to at least upgrade my civilian clothes. Before I left for the Army, I had just bought my first "Flair" legged pants. Bellbottoms had become the norm a year or so prior, but my conservative upbringing left me lagging behind the popular styles.

I went to the mall that had been built while I was gone in a field we used to hunt in when we were kids. I went into a store called Chess King and found some "groovy" bellbottom pants, hip-huggers of course, and some shirts to match. Now I felt a part of the "scene", and hoped I didn't stand out as much.

There were parties almost every night that I was home on leave, and I loved being back with my family and friends. One night Rory and I were walking out of his apartment, crossing the parking lot to his car, when all of a sudden, "Bang...Bang...Bang...Bang..Bang...Bang...Bang" sounded like a machine gun. It turns out that someone with firecrackers at the other end of the parking lot had lit a string of them, not even knowing we were out there. As Rory turned back to where I was, he started to say, "Man, I'll bet that freaked you out...Dick...Dick", he said as he looked for me. Meantime, I was already under a car trying to figure out where my rifle was. Rory spotted me and said, "Wow, man, I guess that did freak you out!" As I realized what had happened, I crawled out from under the car. On the first "Bang", I had hit the ground and started a low crawl to the nearest cover. I got up and noticed my pants were ripped, and I was bleeding on one knee from crawling on the blacktop. I then understood it was going to take me a while to adjust.

My second or third day home I decided to buy my first new car. I had thought in Vietnam that I wanted a Plymouth GTS, but after looking at them I decided they were too rich for my blood. My brother had come home to see me, and took me to look at a Dodge Challenger. He was partial to Dodge because he bought a 1968 Super Bee when he got home from Nam. I liked the Challenger, but it was a new 1970 model, and we found a new 1971 Plymouth Duster for the same money, so I bought it. I was attempting to fit into the "long hair" culture of the day, with its bright colors and "Tie-dies", and so I bought a dark purple Plymouth Duster. The color was called, "In-Violet", and I thought this is my stab at being "Hip". At any rate, I was appalled at the price tag of $2,900.00 for a new car; outrageous!

Seeing my old friends, going to our church, and stopping when and where I wanted to eat at a restaurant, and even driving a car again had become real treats for me having been away from this for so long. On Thanksgiving Day, it had been a tradition for my brothers and I to go hunting. On this Thanksgiving Day, my brother John woke me up early and said "Get up, we're going hunting". "I don't know John", I said, "I'm pretty tired of hunting". He smiled at me and said, "It's ok, here they don't shoot back at you"! I reluctantly agreed to go, and got ready.

John had called a few friends to also go, and we met in some field out in the country. We all walked on line as we crossed the cut cornfields, and I walked on the far right, with my shotgun hanging down at my side. As rabbits or quail would scare up, it seemed they came out in front of us down the line. Everyone would shoot in the traditional manner, and hit some game and not hit some. When the game got to my side of the line, I would lift my shotgun from my hip and hit anything I shot at. John was amazed at what a good shot I had become, and I reminded him that where I had been, you better learn to be a great shot or you're dead.

That Sunday after Thanksgiving Day I had to leave for Ft. Riley, Kansas, as I still had seven months of active duty left before I could get out of the Army. I left early that morning in my Duster for the ten-hour drive to Ft. Riley, Kansas. Ft. Riley was Gen. George Armstrong Custer's Fort, in the middle of the prairie. The main fort was in one place, and all the returning infantry from Vietnam were placed a few miles away from the main fort on what was called Custer's Hill. We were told it was because they considered returning infantry from Vietnam to be nuts and dangerous. I'm sure that was just an old Sergeant's tale, but I did meet some that fit the bill while I was there. I reported into my company late that day, and got my stuff squared away.

Monday morning we fell out for reveille', in the snow at seven am, and were told to get our winter combat gear together. The battalion was going out on the prairie for combat maneuvers for a week. I couldn't believe my ears. We headed out in the snow for war games. I slept out in a tent for one night, and froze by butt off. There were about eight inches of snow and a howling wind that the black guys called "The Hawk", making the wind chill below zero.

I had heard someone talking about the company clerk just getting orders for Vietnam. The wheels began to spin and as the lunch truck was pulling away from the area, I snuck around the tent, and ran up and jumped in the back of it. I got out back in the company area, and walked into the orderly room. The First Sergeant looked up at me and said, "McBain, what are you doing in here"? "Top", I said, "I hear you need a company clerk, and I'm your man!" "What qualifies you for the job", he snarled, "You're a grunt!" "Top, before I was a grunt I was a college student, and happen to have done some orderly room clerking in Vietnam. I know how to do the morning report, the AR's, and can type", I said. "You can do the morning report and the AR's?" he asked. OK, I'll give you a shot, but if you mess up, back you go", he replied.

I knew bringing up the ability to do the morning report would be an attention grabber. I had found out in Vietnam, when I did some orderly room clerking between my medevac and going on R&R that the morning report was absolutely necessary to be done in a certain way and correctly. Many clerks just didn't seem to get it right which was usually taken out on the First Sergeant, so I learned to do it correctly while there, knowing it may be of some use to me later. Morning Reports and AR's (Army Regulations) were hot spots for First Sergeants because they both had to be done a certain way and I could do them.

Now I was just trying to get out of the war games in the snow, but there were a lot more benefits to being the company clerk than I thought. I worked a regular shift; got out of the big bay area with all the guys and into a private room with one other sergeant; and did not have to pull any more guard duty. This turned out to be the best move I had ever made while in the military. Not only that, but the NCO I roomed with was an old friend from basic training, Ed Blaize, and we renewed our friendship quickly. Ed was assigned as the "Re-Enlistment" NCO for the company. His job was to get soldiers to reenlist in the Army for four more years. He and I were both just finishing out our time, and every time someone would come to his office to "re-up", he'd call me at the orderly room, and I'd come down and help him talk them out of it.

I learned how to do "Early-Outs", which was a voluminous amount of paperwork and required knowing regulations in detail. I learned the procedures to get myself a three month early out to go back to college, but as word got around, even to other companies that I could do them, I was approached by several people to do theirs for them. I managed to pick up a few nice gifts for the help, but was happy to get anyone out early that I could.

I applied and received a three-month early out to go back to Miami University. My sister-in-law, Sylvia (Loling) McBain, John's wife, was instrumental in helping me get out early. The VA had messed up my eligibility requirements that I needed for school, and the only way it was going to get done was for someone to go get it. Loling went out of town and got the certificate, and I turned it in just in the nick of time. I left the Army on March 19, 1971.

As I left the fort I was flying in my car with a ten hour drive before me. I was hauling up Interstate 70 when I looked a mile up the road and up the hill and saw several police cars on both sides of my side of the highway. I wondered what had happened. As I got closer they were motioning to me to pull over. As I stopped they approached me and I rolled my window down. Then I heard a chopper go over my car, and I said "what's going on officer?" He asked me for my license and registration and wondered if I knew how fast I was going. Before I answered he said ninety-five. That Army chopper called ahead and warned us that you were speeding excessively when you left Ft Riley, and has been following you. I began to realize I was in trouble, so I played the returning vet card.

"Gosh, I'm sorry officers, I just got back from a year in combat in Vietnam and was heading home to see my folks", I began. "I am so excited about getting home I guess I wasn't paying any attention to my speed; I'm really sorry sir", I exclaimed respectfully. "You're just back from Vietnam?" he asked. "Yes sir, and I have just had home on my mind all morning, and should have been paying attention but wasn't", I said.

They walked away from the car and spoke between themselves for a minute then came back and said, "OK, we're going to just give you a verbal warning this time", he said while handing back my license and registration, "but slow down and live; you've earned it!" "Thank you so much officers, I really appreciate this", I responded.

They waited for me to get going again and I was a speed limit guy all the way to the next exit where they got off. Then it was pedal to the medal all the way home. I just couldn't help myself…I wanted to get home!

CHAPTER TWENTY-THREE

BROTHERS IN BATTLE

One of the things about the army, especially in combat when you are dependent upon each other to survive, is the way preconceived ideas and prejudices seem to disappear. Each unit had a vast array of people with backgrounds that one would rarely have the opportunity to know unless thrown in a situation like war.

In this chapter I have pictures and commentary about my combat brothers and friends. All of them are very special to me because we risked our lives together to serve our country. Many of us were not believers in this war, but all of us were believers in our country. We served because we were either called or decided on our own to do what we could for God, Honor, and Country.

What I have to say about them all, is that it was my honor to know them, to serve with them, and to be a band of brothers that will remain deep in each other's hearts for the rest of our lives. I do not have them in any particular order, and many of them are mentioned or storied in this book. To those brothers of all of us in the 101st Airborne Division, as well as all brothers and sisters who served in Vietnam in any capacity, may God Bless and Keep you and yours forever!

NEWTON "STEVE" CLEMENT – KIA

Steve Clement's medals and awards, including CIB, Bronze Star, Arcom, NDS, VNS, VNC as posted on the Virtual Wall on line

Newton Steve Clement, was originally from Arkansas but had been living in New Mexico, and was my best friend until he was killed. A reliable and friendly guy who was married and had a child he was never able to see.

Steve Clement was funny and light hearted, and he liked people. He was a good soldier and someone you could trust. The way he lost his life was a horrific tragedy as it was due to someone playing around with an explosive item in an ammo dump, of all places.

Everyone that knew Steve was grieved at this terrible accident that took our friend away. May he rest in peace, and may his family find solace that he is in heaven.

Sgt. Tom Brennan was a good guy who was serious about his leading while watching out for his men

Tom Brennan, a fair skinned red headed Nebraskan farmer, who was my squad leader for a few months. Tom was someone I trusted and had some harrowing experiences with on Hill 882.

He came to the company from NCOIC School, where he became a Sergeant E-5. Tom was easy going but did a great job as a squad leader. Men liked Tom and did what he asked without question. He was a straight shooter and you could always believe what he told you.

Willie Thomas and Billy Lyman got to the unit the same day as Dick that led to an immediate camaraderie amongst the three

Willie Thomas, a black soldier from Valdosta Georgia, and Billy Lyman from Missouri had both come to the company the same day as I. Willie had been wounded by the land mine I stepped over, and it was he that yelled at me the warning about my being in a possible mine field. Willie was also shot in the leg while sitting in the door of a helicopter bringing him out to the company from his recovered wounds, but he was ok.

Billy Lyman was a mild manner type guy who was a good friend and dependable. It was he and Willie who opened fire on the enemy coming up on our Christmas LZ, and unnecessarily blaming each other for not killing them. It was their first experience seeing the enemy face to face and ended up with a lot of firing and no one killed.

The three of us were often in the same squad together and were good buddies who trusted one another, and could joke around with one another without someone being offended. Willie was another one of us that used to laugh hard at Reyes's antics. Having good belly laughs in the boonies was not a regular thing but sure could relieve tension. When Willie would give me the "Pound", he would say "Bip" in each hit of the fist, so it was "bip…bip…bip" and so on.

Bill Nelson and Joe Gagliardi were both from Brooklyn, or at least had that type of accent

Bill Nelson and "Little" Joe Gagliardi were from New York and had the accent to prove it. Both of these guys you were happy to have around as they had a great sense of humor and the drive to get things done. Bill was a machine gunner and Little Joe a rifleman.

It was strange because both were in different squads than I was, but I got to know Bill a little better than Joe. I think the reason was that Bill went out of his way when I was a new "Cherry" to try and make me feel at home in the unit. He approached me and would explain things about the operation, or how to do something; I really appreciated that.

Little Joe was more of a quiet guy, and we talked from time to time, but mostly small talk. He was wounded in a friendly-fire incident but was ok.

Staff Sargent's Hunter & Diaz were good leaders and watched out for the men. We could joke around with them until it was serious time with the enemy in close proximity; then there was no joking

SSG. Hunter was a career soldier, and a darn good one. When he directed you to do something you knew he was a man who knew his stuff, and we would comply without question. When things were quiet in the area, he was not as serious, and would joke around with us.

SSG. Diaz, a Puerto Rican who had formerly been a New York pimp before coming into the Army, was a platoon sergeant. Though I didn't know him very well, he also was a good soldier, and one you could have fun with when it was appropriate. He always used to start what he was going to say with, "Dig it man", which seemed apropos for the times.

Wayne "Smitty" Smith was a mild manner man who would give you the shirt off of his back and always spoke softly, which had a calming effect

Wayne Smith was a great guy who was always willing to help with whatever was needed. "Smitty" as we called him was a machine-gunner and one of the crowd, being a quiet personality. He was regrettably killed on Hill 882.

Farrel "Caje" Faul was a good soldier you could rely on. When he left country six months before me, he was noticeably missed

Farrel Faul was a Cajun from bayou country in Louisiana, and carried an M-60 machine gun. He was always called "Caje", and I loved his accent. He could be funny at times if you could decipher his thick bayou country dialect. However, if you got on his wrong side you would hear, "Hey man, you no wanna do dat"

The Chicago Boys, Muff Andrews, Richard Hayman, and Sgt. Nyman in Camp Eagle during a stand-down

"Muff" Andrews, Richard Hayman, and Sgt. Ray Nyman were from Chicago. Ray was a squad leader, then a platoon sergeant, and was with the guys who pulled us out of being pinned down on Hill 882. He was a good soldier.

Richard carried a radio like me. We both were willing to carry the extra weight of a radio so we could always be in contact, and know what was going on. Richard was funny and liked to joke like I did.

"Muff" was a rifleman, and one of the guys who was fun to be around.

Lt. Greg Morehead was another "Child" looking man, but a good leader. He looked after his men with direction and compassion. Ed Matajesyk was another mild-mannered man and served as Lt. Morehead's RTO

Lt. Greg Morehead was my first platoon leader, and Ed Matejesyk, his RTO, were good guys you could always talk to. Lt. Morehead, after serving his time in the jungle, got a rear job. His jeep hit a land mine and he was thrown twenty-five feet but survived, and his driver was critically injured.

Ed got robbed by the village kids when he was getting ready to leave for Hawaii on R&R to meet his wife.

John Gutekunst, KIA, Richard Hayman, and "Shorty"

John Gutekunst was from Philly, and was one of the guys who annoyed me with the "Cherry" term when I first arrived at the company. We soon became friends, and he was later killed by a friendly fire incident. Also pictured are Richard Hayman and "Shorty" from Oklahoma.

Richard and I used to joke around with, and about the radios from time to time, such as one saying to another, "What the hell…are you stupid carrying all that extra weight?" Of course we both carried the radio.

Shorty was always Thomas' (point-man) side kick. They could have had a sitcom together.

"Top" Manning was an experienced leader who was nearly killed on Hill 882 when the enemy shot at him and hit him in the helmet, but the bullet ricochet off

First Sergeant Manning who was a great leader and took care of his troops was tough but friendly. He later became the company First Sargent during the battle of Hill 882.

John Ridgeway came to the company after I had been there a while. He later went home after re-upping

Doc Minks & Doc Shenk were always running around making sure everyone had their heat tabs, and mosquito pills. They took care of all of the cuts and scrapes, as well as running out under fire to the wounded

Doc Minks and Doc Bill Shenk were Medic's in our company. Doc Minks was the CP Medic, and Doc Shenk was from Kansas City, Missouri who in my mind was a hero of hero's. Doc Shenk was there under fire when someone got hit, and I'll never forget his run up the hill to our ammo dump in Camp Eagle while it was exploding all around him, to get Steve Clement out of there.

SSG Johnson was one of the senior experienced leaders who was always watching out for others, and pal'd around with Doc Shenk and me

SSG Lonnie Johnson was a career soldier and one of the best I ever saw in a firefight. He was the kind of guy you wanted with you when trouble came because he instinctively knew what to do, and then did it. He used my knife to save me from a deadly snake bite. He became a real buddy of mine, along with Doc Bill Shenk. Whenever we would get to the rear on a stand-down, he and Doc would come looking for me. When they found me it was, "Mac, we gotta get drunk". We did tie some on together, but in the boonies both were the best of the best.

Lt. Roy Richardson - KIA
1st Lt. Roy Richardson

Lt. Roy Richardson was an Airborne Ranger who became our platoon leader when Lt. Morehead received a rear job. He was a Mormon, and one of the nicest people you could meet. He was tough as nails but with a gentleness that made you want to follow him. He was killed beside me on Hill 882 and awarded the Distinguished Service Cross Posthumously.

Dennis Buckingham checking out a slide he had processed from his camera.

Dennis Buckingham was from California, and one of the guys who broke through under fire to get us out of our pinned down situation on Hill 882.

Sgt. Bishop was a good soldier who would get flustered at Reyes's antics, and Reyes would just continue to fluster him

Waddel Bishop was an early squad leader of mine, and taught me things I needed to know to survive.

OTHER BROTHERS IN OUR UNIT

"Crazy J" Jenetta and Robert Van Pala on a training break during a stand-down joke around

Joe Russo, Jim Henson, Dick, and LT. Hubbard chilling out and hanging together shooting the breeze

Sonny Gordon & Joe Cymbulista in Camp Eagle during a stand-down

SP4 Bankus writing a letter home in the jungle

"Shark", the only name I ever heard him called, and Oliver "Jeff" Jefferson at their NDP position in the jungle

Mel De Voss was from Indiana and Dick was from neighboring Ohio, and we spoke a lot about our Midwest upbringing

Larry Dent was a brother who tried to play the tough guy but was a lot of fun and good friend

Jaco and Joe joking around on a stand-down at Camp Eagle

"Boonie-Rats" set up in the jungle for business. Mortar tube in forefront, with a trooper holing his M-79 "Thumper", while others check out the area

Stand-down training break outside of Camp Eagle, and a "Chinook" Chopper bringing artillery ammo to a Firebase

Dick with enemy cache & Stroh's beer from home. He is holding a light enemy machinegun captured with various other weapons and ammunition, with an enemy RPG (Rocket Propelled Grenade) launcher and rounds in the forefront

Sgt. Tom Brennan & "Shark" taking a break after blowing an LZ with dynamite for a resupply. Our unit carried a four day resupply, and needed to either find an already blown LZ or blow a new one every four days

"Top" Manning had been our Field First Sergeant until after the Battle of Hill 882. He then was promoted to Company A's First Sergeant

Sgt. Tom Brennan with Scout Dog that would be sent out to us from time to time to "sniff" out the enemy. Richard Hayman in front of his poncho hooch with a M-79 grenade launcher

Sgt. Diaz, Dick, Billy Lyman and others clowning around while waiting to be picked up by choppers for a CA (Combat Assault) into their next AO (Area of Operations)

Richard Hayman, Top Manning, Dick, and Sgt. Stansfield hanging out on a FSB (Fire Support Base)

Mel De Voss from Indiana, and Joe Gagliardi from Brooklyn off duty in Camp Eagle, and several of the men at a FSB Gun Position

Football during a stand-down was a way to have fun and release pent up hostility in a recreational way. The graves of the losing team cannot be seen at the left (just kidding)

Ed Matajesyk repairing his liner from under his Poncho shelter in the jungle. Guys looking down from chopper as they prepare to land on a fire support base

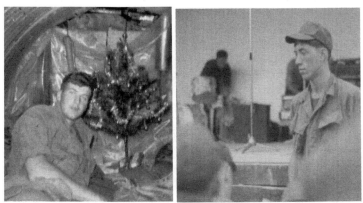

Dick in Lt. Morehead and Ed Matajesyk's hooch on FSB Rifle with Christmas tree in background. John Gutekunst in front of the stage at a stand-down while band prepares for evening show

Troop sitting atop a Fire Support Base border position, reading the Stars & Stripes, a military newspaper. The sand bags on top provided cover for shooters on top as well as down below

Joe, Jaco & "Blondie" in a cleared out defensive position, with an M-60 machine gun and ammo at right.

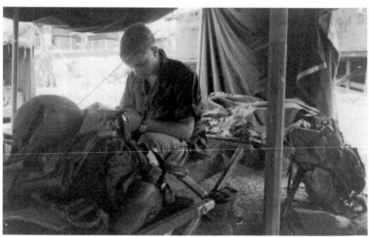

Don Cordle reading while waiting to go on the next mission after a stand-down. The packed rucksacks show the readiness to head out, and exemplify what we carried on our backs on missions

"Blondie" and "Wolf" at a cleared defensive position in the jungle. Waiting was so many times SOP and was welcome at times and an annoyance at others

Willie Thomas, Sonny Gordon, Joe Cymbulista, and Willie Wilcox at a FSB position. Willie Thomas came in-country the same day as I did, and became a good friend. Notice Joe having the two bottles of "Bug Juice" strapped to his helmet. These were very much needed for mosquitoes and leaches

Some of the guys sitting in a clearing in the jungle talking and passing the time while others not seen cover them from their defensive positions

"Shorty" & Diep on a FSB having a hot breakfast. Sgt. Steve Clement in the field with a trooper he is instructing about setting up a defensive position

SSG Lonnie Johnson is showing the direction the platoon will be moving on the map. The detail on the map was critical to move in triple canopy jungle, and was still hard to follow because landmarks were hard to see.

Steve Clément's grave headstone. He was married before going to Vietnam, and they had a baby while he was there that he never saw.

Don Cordle loaded up and moving out. Don had a rucksack like Dick's with the extra weight of the PRC radio, and lots of water. See the five quart blivit canteen on top. These also made good pillows in the jungle

101st Airborne Patch – Strike Force – Widow Maker Patch

Dick with BJ his dog at the Vietnam Veterans Memorial in Washington, D.C., in late October 1986. Dick has been to "The Wall" many times over the years and is moved with emotion and gratitude for all of those who made the supreme sacrifice in a war that so many were against.

NOT PICTURED

Mathew Smith, also referred to as "Smitty" was from Massachusetts, and had been in the Hell's Angels before coming into the Army. He was seriously injured on Hill 882 while walking point.

Peter Nolan - Killed on Hill 882

Michael Ledden, served with us in the field before he became our Company Clerk.

EPILOGUE

After the war I spent some time trying to fit into a culture I didn't like much. I was very fortunate because I never experienced PTSD, and it was only a little matter of time that I needed to adjust back to civilian life. I met my wife Jackie a little over a year after my discharge from the Army, and as of this writing have been married forty-two years.

I find it funny that most of the college demonstrators against the war and the government establishment, have all settled in to the same middle class life they were brought up in. The thing most different from their parent's generation is that they have in great numbers remained in the selfish mode.

Most Baby-boomer couples have decided to both work outside the home so they can have nicer things, and the big losers are their children. There should be no doubt that the family as a social unit has been decimated from being the cohesive element in our culture, and is explained as "I did it for them". Sure you did, while you drive your Beemer's and live in big houses, the children suffer for loss of love, attention, and proper training.

America is still the best country in the world, but a big slice of the American people have gone the way of the world, instead of the way God intended. Of course, many don't even believe in God anymore so we shouldn't be surprised.

I finish with a salute to all of my brothers and sisters who served in Vietnam, and who have and do serve this great country in any capacity. You are the best of us!

VIET NAM WAR GLOSSARY

Airmobile – units that move by helicopter
AO – Area of Operations
Bee-hive Round – Artillery type shot-gun shell with "Fleshette" arrows in them
Blivit – Small or large hard rubber cylinder container for water or gas
Blue-line – river, stream, creek
C's (Charlie Rats) – C Rations
CA – Combat Assault by Helicopter
Cache' – A compilation of enemy weapons, guns, and ammunition
Charlie (Chuck) – Enemy VC or NVA Soldier
Chou-hoi – Surrender
CIB – Combat Infantryman's Badge – earned after being in actual combat
Claymore Mine – Directional above ground anti-personnel weapon with C-4 explosive behind 700 steel balls
Cluster –f_k - soldiers grouped together making a better target
Cobra – Bell AH-1 Cora Gunship 2 seat helicopter, that could dive at two hundred miles per hour while firing two different mini-guns and two rocket launchers
Daisy-chain – connecting multiple explosives with Det-cord
Der it is breeze – term used by soldiers meaning that's the way it is
Det Cord – An explosive fuse exploding at 4 miles per second, used to daisy-chain multiple explosives
Di Di Mau – leave now, quickly, get out of my face
Dink – Enemy, bad guy

Dust-off – (Medevac) – Extracting wounded by helicopter
Extraction – Removal of individuals or units out of an AO by helicopter
FSB – Fire Support Base – hill blown clear at top for artillery supporting the troops in the AO
Gook – Vietnamese person including the enemy
HE – Highly Explosive artillery round
Kit Carson Scouts – former enemy combatants who chou-hoi'd and became scouts for us
Loach – Bell LOH Helicopter, used for Command and Control, and sometimes equipped with a mini-gun
LRRP's (Lerps) – Long Range Recon Patrol – Freeze dried meals in plastic bags – light weight and just add water
LZ – Landing Zone where choppers could land
Mini-gun – Gatling revolving six barrel gun firing 2,000 to 6,000 7.62 mm rounds per minute, literally cutting down anything in its path
Number One – Good, best
Number Ten – Bad, worst
One Twenty-twos – Enemy rockets with 10 mile range, usually used to attack base camps and firebases
POS – Position you were at or in
Puff (the magic dragon) – also known as "Spooky" was an Air Force AC-47 Gunship, utilizing civilian version of the DC-3 airplane with three mini-guns firing out one side while the plane is leaning the way the guns are firing, usually in support of ground troops
Pungi stake – excrement covered bamboo spears, usually sunk at the bottom of a pit, or pungi-pit where a soldier would fall in and be impaled by the stakes. If still alive, the excrement could cause serious infection
Red-ball – large cleared path or road in the jungle
Red-leg (Arty) – Artillery unit nickname

Slack-jump – troops jump out of helicopter on a rope and free fall the length of slack they let out before rope grabs, then let themselves down to the ground

Slick – Huey UH-1D Helicopter was mostly used for troop movement, including CA's (Combat Assaults) and Medical Evacuation (Medevac)

Smoke-Bringer – Code for Phantom Jets or Helicopter Gunships that would do just that

Thumper – M-79 Grenade Launcher, breach open, single shot grenade round that looked like a large bullet

Trip-flare – Metal encased flare to attach to a tree and connect to a trip wire, or pull pin and throw like a grenade

WP (Willie Peter) – White Phosphorous artillery round or grenade

SOME VIETNAM STATISTICS
As Reported by the Mobile Riverine Force Association
http://www.mrfa.org/

PERSONNEL

9,087,000 military personnel served on active duty during the Vietnam Era (5 August 1965-7 May 1975)

8,744,000 personnel were on active duty during the war (5 August 1964-28 March 1973) 3,403,100 (including 514,300 offshore) personnel served in the SE Asia Theater (Vietnam, Laos, Cambodia, flight crews based in Thailand and sailors in adjacent South China Sea waters).

2,594,000 personnel served within the borders of South Vietnam (I January 1965 - 28 March 1973) Another 50,000 men served in Vietnam between 1960 and 1964

Of the 2.6 million, between 1 and 1.6 million (40-60%) either fought in combat, provided close combat support or were at least fairly regularly exposed to enemy attack.

7,484 women served in Vietnam, of whom 6,250 or 83.5% were nurses. Peak troop strength in Vietnam was 543,482, on 30 April 1969.

CASUALTIES

Hostile deaths: 47,359 - Non-hostile deaths: 10,797 Total: 58,156 (including men formerly classified as MIA and Mayaguez casualties).

Highest state death rate: West Virginia--84.1. (The national average death rate for males in 1970 was 58.9 per 100,000).

WIA: 303,704 - 153,329 required hospitalization, 50,375 who did not.

Severely disabled: 75,000 - 23,214 were classified 100% disabled - 5,283 lost limbs - 1,081 sustained multiple amputations. Amputation or crippling wounds to the lower extremities were 300% higher than in WWII and 70% higher than in Korea. Multiple amputations occurred at the rate of 18.4% compared to 5.7% in WWII.

MIA: 2,338

POW: 766, of whom 114 died in captivity.

Draftees vs. volunteers:
25% (648,500) of total forces in country were draftees.

(66% of U.S. armed forces members were drafted during WWII)

Draftees accounted for 30.4% (17,725) of combat deaths in Vietnam. Reservists KIA: 5,977 National Guard: 6,140 served; 101 died.

ETHNIC BACKGROUND

88.4% of the men who actually served in Vietnam were Caucasian

10.6% (275,000) were black

1.0% belonged to other races

86.3% of the men who died in Vietnam were Caucasian (including Hispanics)

12.5% (7,241) were black.

1.2% belonged to other races

170,000 Hispanics served in Vietnam; 3,070 (5.2%) of whom died there.

86.8% of the men who were KIA were Caucasian

12.1% (5,711) were black

1.1% belonged to other races

14.6% (1,530) of non-combat deaths were black 34% of blacks who enlisted volunteered for the combat arms. Overall, blacks suffered 12.5% of the deaths in Vietnam when the percentage of blacks of military age was 13.5% of the population.

SOCIOECONOMIC STATUS

76% of the men sent to Vietnam were from lower middle/working class backgrounds

75% had family incomes above the poverty level

23% had fathers with professional, managerial, or technical occupations.

79% of the men who served in 'Nam had a high school education or better.

WINNING & LOSING
82% of veterans who saw heavy combat strongly believe the war was lost because of a lack of political will.

Nearly 75% of the general public (in 1993) agrees with that.

AGE & HONORABLE SERVICE

The average age of the G.I. in 'Nam was 19 (26 for WWII) 97% of Vietnam era vets were honorably discharged.

PRIDE IN SERVICE

91% of veterans of actual combat and 90% of those who saw heavy combat are proud to have served their country. 66% of Viet vets say they would serve again, if called upon. 87% of the public now holds Viet vets in high esteem.

Helicopter crew deaths accounted for 10% of ALL Vietnam deaths. Helicopter losses during Lam Son 719 (a mere two months) accounted for 10% of all helicopter losses from 1961-1975.

*America – Land of the Free
Because of the Brave!*

ACKNOWLEDGEMENTS

Bill Nelson – Many photographs and corroborating some information

Richard Hayman – Many photographs and corroborating some information

Dennis Buckingham – Corroborating some information

Greg Morehead – Corroborating some information

Don Cordle - Pictures

Phillip Nordyke – Encouragement to write the book and help with the publishing

Mobile Riverine Force Association – War Stats

Made in the USA
Middletown, DE
19 October 2015